# SPECTRUM

# Language Arts

# Grade 3

Published by Spectrum®
an imprint of Carson-Dellosa Publishing LLC
Greensboro, NC

Spectrum®
An imprint of Carson-Dellosa Publishing LLC
P.O. Box 35665
Greensboro, NC 27425  USA

Printed in the USA • All rights reserved.          ISBN 978-1-4838-1206-9

01-227147811

# Table of Contents Grade 3

# Table of Contents, continued

## Table of Contents, continued

### Chapter 4 Writer's Guide

A **common noun** can be a person, place, or thing.

*teacher* (person)　　　　　　*museum* (place)
*notebook* (thing)

A **proper noun** is a noun that names a specific person, place, or thing. Proper nouns are capitalized to show that they are important.

Here are some examples of common and proper nouns:

| Common Nouns | Proper Nouns |
| --- | --- |
| school | Hickory Hills Elementary School |
| zoo | Memphis Zoo |
| brother | Alexander |
| city | Tallahassee |
| day | Sunday |
| cat | Sasha |

**Complete It**

Complete the sentences below with a noun from the box. If there is a **P** after the space, use a proper noun. If there is a **C** after the space, use a common noun.

| Walnut High School | Saturday | town |
| --- | --- | --- |
| dog | Jordan Lake | brother |

1. Uncle Dale is taking me fishing at _Jordan Lake_ (P).

2. We will leave early on _Saturday_ (P) morning.

3. My _brother_ (C), Kris, is coming with us.

4. Uncle Dale lives an hour away in a _town_ (C) called Rockvale.

5. He is a math teacher at _Walnut High School_ (P).

6. Uncle Dale's _dog_ (C), Patches, always comes fishing with us.

## Lesson 1.1   Common and Proper Nouns

**Identify It**

Underline the nouns in the sentences below. The number in parentheses will tell you how many nouns there are. Above each noun, write **P** for *proper* or **C** for *common*.

1. Patches jumped into the rowboat. (2)

2. Kris and I put on our life jackets. (2)

3. Last August, we went to Griggs Lake. (2)

4. We stopped at Elmwood Historic Car Museum on the way home. (2)

5. We caught six fish on our trip. (2)

6. Uncle Dale cooked them on the grill. (2)

7. Mom made some coleslaw and potatoes. (3)

**Try It**

1. Write a sentence using at least two common nouns. Circle the nouns.

   _____

   _____

2. Write a sentence using two proper nouns and one common noun. Circle the common noun. Underline the proper nouns.

   _____

   _____

# Lesson 1.2   Abstract Nouns

**Abstract nouns** are nouns that you can't experience with your five senses. They are feelings, concepts, and ideas. Some examples are *friendship, childhood, bravery, hope,* and *pride.*

## Identify It

Underline the abstract noun or nouns in each sentence below.

1. Maya's honesty is one of the reasons we are best friends.

2. Martin Luther King, Jr., wanted to change hate and injustice in the world.

3. Darius's patriotism is the reason he joined the army.

4. I love the delight on my sister's face on her birthday.

5. Your kindness will not be forgotten.

6. Benji felt great pride when his team won the championship.

7. What are your parents' best stories about their childhood?

8. It is important to me that you always tell the truth.

## Lesson 1.2 | Abstract Nouns

### Complete It

Fill in each blank below with an abstract noun from the box.

| wisdom | liberty | freedom | knowledge |
|--------|---------|---------|-----------|
| courage | joy | kindness | |

1. Our country was founded on the ideas of _____ and _____ for all.

2. It took great _____ to rebuild after the hurricane.

3. Uncle Zane's _____ of birds amazes me.

4. The room was filled with _____ when Will found his lost puppy.

5. Neighbors showed us much _____ when my baby sister was born.

6. Grandpa has the _____ that comes with a long life.

### Try It

Write three sentences that use abstract nouns. You may use abstract nouns from the exercises or think of your own.

1. _____

2. _____

3. _____

## Lesson 1.3  Pronouns

A **pronoun** is a word that takes the place of a noun. Pronouns keep you from using the same noun or nouns over and over again.

Some pronouns take the place of a single person or thing: *I, me, you, he, she, him, her,* and *it.* Other pronouns take the place of plural nouns: *we, us, they,* and *them.*

In the examples below, pronouns take the place of the underlined nouns.

> The grizzly bears waded into the stream.
> *They* waded into the stream.
> Molly finished her report at noon.
> *She* finished her report at noon.
> Put the bowl on the table.
> Put *it* on the table.

**Identify It**

Read the paragraphs below. Circle each pronoun. You should find 15 pronouns.

Sonja Henie was an amazing figure skater. She was born in Oslo, Norway, in 1912. When Sonja was only five years old, she won her first skating contest. It was the start of a great career. She was a world champion for ten years. People around the world became interested in skating. They followed the career of the talented young girl.

Sonja also wanted to be a movie star. She moved to Hollywood and began acting. She also performed in a traveling ice show. It was very popular. Huge crowds came to watch Sonja perform. They could not get enough of her. Sonja enjoyed her fame and the money it brought her. But her first and greatest love was always skating.

## Lesson 1.3 Pronouns

**Rewrite It**

Read the sentences below. Rewrite each sentence using
a pronoun in place of the underlined noun or nouns.

Example: <u>David</u> kicked the ball toward the goal.
*He* kicked the ball toward the goal.

1. <u>Bryan and Anna</u> had their first skating lesson on Tuesday.

_____

2. <u>Bryan</u> had never skated before.

_____

3. <u>The ice</u> was slick and shiny.

_____

4. The teacher helped <u>Anna</u> tighten the skates.

_____

5. The teacher told <u>Bryan and Anna</u> that they did a great job.

_____

**Try It**

1. Think about the first time you tried something new. Write a sentence
about your experience. Circle the pronoun.

_____

2. Write a sentence using the pronoun *he, she,* or *it.*

_____

## Lesson 1.4   Verbs

**Verbs** are often action words. They tell what happens in a sentence. Every sentence has a verb.

Ramon *put* on his running shoes. He *grabbed* his headphones. He *opened* the door and *took* a deep breath. Ramon *stretched* for a few minutes. Then, he *ran* down the street toward the park.

### Complete It

A verb is missing from each sentence below. Complete the sentences with verbs from the box.

| breathed | moved | attached | invented |
|---|---|---|---|
| gave | kept | carried | helped |

1. In 1819, August Siebe _____ the first diving suit.

2. The large helmet _____ to a leather and canvas suit.

3. Weights _____ divers stay underwater.

4. The divers underwater _____ air through hoses.

5. Later on, rubber suits _____ divers dry.

6. The invention of scuba gear _____ divers more freedom.

7. Divers _____ from place to place on their own.

8. They _____ their air with them.

## Lesson 1.4　Verbs

**Identify It**

Circle the 10 action verbs in the paragraphs below.

Jacques Cousteau explored many of Earth's oceans. In 1950, he bought a ship called *Calypso*. On the *Calypso*, Jacques traveled to bodies of water around the world. He wrote many books and made many movies about his travels. He won prizes for some of his work. Jacques also invented things, like an underwater camera and the first scuba equipment.

Jacques Cousteau believed it was important to protect ocean life. He created a group called the *Cousteau Society*. More than 300,000 people belong to the Cousteau Society today.

**Try It**

1. Write a sentence about a place you would like to visit one day. Circle the verb.

_____

_____

_____

2. Write a sentence about your favorite thing to do during the weekend. Circle the verb.

_____

_____

_____

## Lesson 1.5  Linking Verbs

A **linking verb** links the subject to the rest of the sentence. Linking verbs are not action words.

The verb *to be* is a linking verb. Some different forms of the verb *to be* are *is, am, are, was,* and *were*. Some other linking verbs are *become, feel,* and *seem*.

**Identify It**

Read the sentences below. Underline the linking verbs. Circle the action verbs. Some sentences may have more than one verb.

1. My grandmother is a marine biologist.

2. She studies undersea life.

3. She was always a good student.

4. She loved the ocean and animals as a child.

5. It was hard for her to become a scientist.

6. When she was young, some people felt women could not be good at science.

7. My grandma proved she was smart and hardworking.

8. One day, I might become a marine biologist myself.

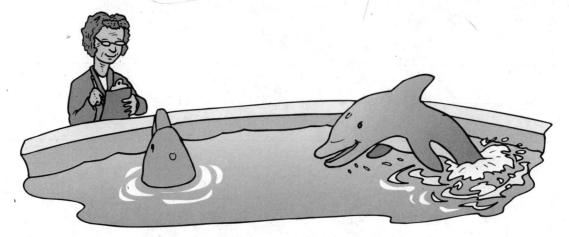

## Lesson 1.5 Linking Verbs

**Solve It**

Use the linking verbs from the box to complete each sentence. Some may work for more than one sentence. Then, look for the linking verbs in the word search puzzle. Circle each word you find.

1. Today, my grandfather _____ a stage actor.

2. He first _____ a movie star at the age of 22.

3. He _____ lucky to have had such an amazing career.

4. I _____ going to see him in a Broadway play next week.

5. When my dad _____ little, he was in one of Grandpa's movies.

| feels | am | |
|-------|----|-----|
| was | is | became |

| a | d | r | j | k | f | p |
|---|---|---|---|---|---|---|
| b | e | c | a | m | e | i |
| d | w | a | s | b | e | y |
| a | f | v | c | u | l | p |
| m | u | f | q | i | s | g |

**Try It**

1. Write a sentence using a linking verb.

_____

_____

2. Write a sentence using a linking verb and an action verb.

_____

_____

## Review   Nouns, Pronouns, and Verbs

**Nouns** name people, places, and things.

  *cousin   doctor   library   plant   sticker*

**Proper nouns** are capitalized. They name specific people, places, or things.

  *Aunt Claudia   Crestview Middle School   Rockefeller Center*

**Abstract nouns** are feelings, concepts, or ideas.

  *charity   hope   friendship   truth   trust   anger*

**Pronouns** can take the place of nouns in a sentence.

  *I   me   you   he   she   him   her   it   we   us   they   them*

Some **verbs** are action words. They tell what happens in a sentence.

  *read   fall   push   fold   laugh   stir*

**Linking verbs** link the subject of a sentence to the rest of the sentence.

  *is   am   are   was   were   become   feel   seem*

### Putting It Together

In each sentence below, circle the verb. Write **L** in the space if it is a linking verb. Write **A** in the space if it is an action verb.

 1. Taipei 101 is the tallest skyscraper in the world. _____

 2. Chicago's Home Insurance Building was the first skyscraper. _____

 3. Many TV stations broadcast from the Empire State Building. _____

 4. Large frames, not walls, support skyscrapers. _____

 5. In 1973, the Willis Tower became the tallest building in the world. _____

Write two sentences using abstract nouns. Circle the abstract noun in each.

_____

_____

## Review   Nouns, Pronouns, and Verbs

Read the paragraphs below. Underline the common nouns. Circle the proper nouns. There are 11 common nouns and 14 proper nouns.

   Tess and her parents visited the Empire State Building. It is located in New York City. The Empire State Building was built in 1930. Only one building in the United States is taller.

   Tess and her parents bought tickets. Then, they took the elevator to the 86th floor. Tess loved seeing the view of the city from the observatory. She felt like she was standing on top of the world. Dad showed her the Hudson River. Mom pointed out Massachusetts, Connecticut, New Jersey, and Pennsylvania.

Read the sentences below. Rewrite each sentence using a pronoun in place of the underlined word or words.

1. The Empire State Building has appeared in many movies.

   _____

2. Tess bought a postcard to send to her grandparents.

   _____

3. On their first date, Tess's parents went to the top of the Empire State Building.

   _____

4. Tess learned that the building gets hit by lightning about 100 times per year.

   _____

## Lesson 1.6  Adjectives and Articles

**Adjectives** are words that describe. They give more information about nouns. Adjectives answer the questions *What kind?* and *How many?* They often come before the nouns they describe.

   Fat raindrops bounced off the umbrella. (what kind of raindrops?)

Adjectives can also appear other places in the sentence. If you are not sure a word is an adjective, look for the noun you think it describes.

   The robot was *helpful*.    The package is *huge*!

An **article** is a word that comes before a noun. *A*, *an*, and *the* are articles.

Use *the* to talk about a specific person, place, or thing.

   *the* computer  *the* jacket  *the* bicycle  *the* starfish

Use *a* or *an* to talk about any person, place, or thing. If the noun begins with a consonant sound, use *a*. If it begins with a vowel sound, use *an*.

   *a* wig  *a* bed  *an* apple  *an* envelope

**Complete It**

Complete each item below with an adjective from the box.

| | | | | |
|---|---|---|---|---|
| shy | electric | ~~prickly~~ | warty | ~~smelly~~ |
| seven | skinny | tiny | howling | wrinkled |

1. the ___Prickly___ porcupine

2. the ___Warty___ toad

3. the ___electric___ eel

4. the gray, ___wrinkled___ elephant

5. the ___tiny___ hummingbird

6. the tall, ___Skinny___ giraffe

7. the ___Smelly___ skunk

8. the ___Shy___ deer

9. the ___howling___ wolf

10. ___Seven___ flamingos

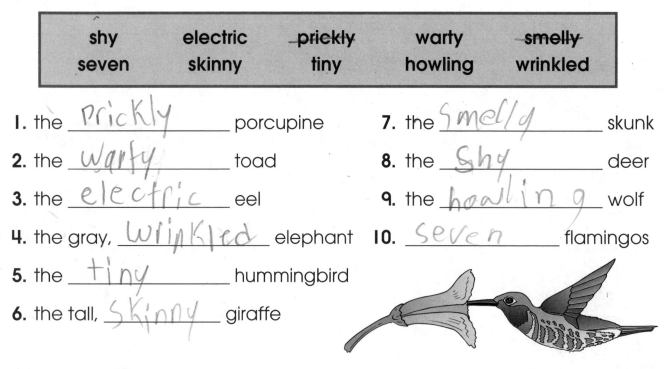

## Lesson 1.6 Adjectives and Articles

**Rewrite It**

The sentences below do not give the reader much information. Rewrite the sentences. Add at least two adjectives to each sentence.

I. The dog barked at the squirrel as it ran up the tree.

_____

_____

2. The dolphin dove into the waves and swam toward the sunset.

_____

_____

**Proof It**

Read the paragraph below. Circle the 20 articles you find. Six of the articles are incorrect. Cross them out, and write the correct articles above them.

A time capsule is a interesting way to communicate with people in a future. A time capsule is a group of items from the present time. An items tell something about a person, a place, or a moment in time. They are sealed in a container. A glass jar or the plastic box with a tight lid works well. Then, the capsule is buried or put in an safe place. An attached note should say when the capsule will be opened. Some capsules are opened in the year or in ten years. Others will stay buried or hidden for a thousand or even five thousand years!

# Lesson 1.7  Adverbs

**Adverbs** are words that describe verbs. Adverbs often answer the questions *When? Where?* or *How?*

She *joyfully* cheered for them.    *Joyfully* tells *how* she cheered.

*Yesterday*, I had a picnic.    *Yesterday* tells *when* I had a picnic.

Brady put the box *downstairs*.    *Downstairs* tells *where* Brady put the box.

Adverbs can also describe adjectives. They usually answer the question *How?*

Sierra was **too** late.    The sunset was **really** beautiful.

Adverbs can describe other adverbs, too.

Luke spoke **extremely** quietly.    Shawn **very** sadly said good-bye.

## Complete It

An adverb is missing from each sentence below. Choose the adverb from the box that best completes each sentence. Write it on the line. Then, circle the word the adverb describes.

| | | |
|---|---|---|
| **loudly** | **brightly** | **often** |
| **beside** | **suddenly** | **completely** |

1. Dylan sat _____ Amina at the school play.

2. The two friends _____ went to plays together.

3. The room was _____ dark.

4. _____, the curtain opened.

5. The scenery onstage was _____ painted.

6. The children said their lines _____ so that everyone could hear them.

## Lesson 1.7    Adverbs

### Solve It

Read the sentences below. Find the adverb in each sentence. Write it on the lines after the sentence.

1. The prince slowly climbed Rapunzel's long hair.

____ ____ ◯ ____ ____

2. Little Red Riding Hood safely returned home.

◯ ____ ____ ____ ____

3. The wolf hid outside. ◯ ____ ____ ____ ____ ____ ____

4. Jack climbed down the beanstalk to escape the giant.

◯ ____ ____ ____

5. The cast proudly bowed at the end of the play.

____ ____ ◯ ____ ____ ____ ____

Write the circled letters from your answers on the lines below.

____ ____ ____ ____ ____

Unscramble the letters to find the missing word in the title of the play.

    Into the _____

### Try It

Write two sentences about a fairy tale. Use an adverb from the box in each sentence. Circle the adverb. Then, underline the word the adverb describes.

| quickly | carefully | softly | completely |
|---------|-----------|--------|------------|
| suddenly | gently | sadly | |

1. _____

2. _____

## Lesson 1.8 Conjunctions

A **conjunction** joins together words, phrases, and parts of sentences. The most common conjunctions are *and, or,* and *but.* Other conjunctions are *since, because, although, if, while, unless,* and *however.*

> Chloe loves Brussels sprouts, *but* Haley won't eat them.
> *Since* you play soccer, can you give me some tips?

**Complete It**

Choose a conjunction to complete each sentence. Write it on the line.

1. Do you want to play the violin _____ the piano? (or, but)

2. Mr. Randall canceled Lucy's lesson _____ he had a cold. (unless, because)

3. Let's play a duet at the recital _____ we can learn it in time. (while, if)

4. Owen plays the drums, _____ Marcus plays the trombone. (and, or)

5. Mrs. Klein likes to knit _____ Ezra practices singing. (however, while)

6. Liam always practices his scales, _____ Alla never does. (but, if)

7. Jade can buy a drum set, _____ her parents want her to help pay for it. (however, or)

8. _____ Vikram's lesson is at 11:00, he often arrives at 10:30. (While, Although)

## Lesson 1.8   Conjunctions

**Rewrite It**

Combine each pair of sentences using a conjunction. There may be more than one correct answer for each item.

**1.** Jack wants to take violin lessons. His sister has been taking them for years.

_____

_____

**2.** Nora plays piano by ear. She can't read notes at all.

_____

_____

**3.** Dion enjoys listening to music. He doesn't play any instruments yet.

_____

_____

**4.** Mr. Santiago hums. He practices every afternoon.

_____

_____

**Try It**

Write a short paragraph about music. Use at least four conjunctions, and circle them.

_____

_____

_____

_____

# Review  Adjectives, Articles, Adverbs, and Conjunctions

**Adjectives** are words that describe nouns. They answer the questions *What kind?* and *How many?*

      The *blue* bicycle had *two shiny* handles and a *loud* bell.

**Adverbs** are words that describe verbs, adjectives, or other adverbs. Adverbs often answer the questions *When?*, *Where?*, or *How?*

      *Yesterday*, Chris left for Tokyo. (when)

      I heard a loud noise *outside*. (where)

*A, an*, and *the* are **articles**. Use *the* to talk about a specific person, place, or thing. Use *a* or *an* to talk about any person, place, or thing.

      *the* button                       *a* mask

**Conjunctions** can join words, phrases, or sentences.

      Mac *and* I are coming for dinner.

      Jordan swims, *but* Milo would rather skate.

## Putting It Together

Underline the adverb in each sentence below. Then, write *when, where,* or *how* in the space to show which question the adverb answers.

1. Carousels are often called *merry-go-rounds*. _____

2. A carousel is a platform that turns slowly in circles. _____

3. Carousels may have first been used 1,500 years ago. _____

4. As a horse moves up, a child may try to grab the brass ring. _____

## Review Adjectives, Articles, Adverbs, and Conjunctions

Read the sentences below. If the underlined word is an adjective, write *adj.* above it. If it is an adverb, write *adv.* above it. If it is a conjunction, write *con.* above it.

adv.
Example: Sophie whispered <u>softly</u> to her little brother.

1. Carousels were very <u>popular</u> in America from about 1885 until 1930.

2. <u>Early</u> carousels were powered with a crank, <u>but</u> this took a lot of work.

3. Carousels were powered <u>later</u> with steam, <u>and</u> then electricity.

4. Carousels could <u>often</u> be found at fairs and amusement parks.

5. <u>Although</u> <u>graceful</u> horses were the most famous, there were also giraffes, tigers, rabbits, and ostriches.

Read the following paragraph. Fill in each space with the article *a*, *an*, or *the*. Circle the nine adjectives you find.

Today, I went to _____ Bushnell Park Carousel in Hartford, Connecticut. It is _____ extremely old carousel. It was built in 1914. I rode _____ beautiful gray horse. It was a jumper horse and had _____ long, flowing mane. My little sister and my mom rode together in _____ chariot. We listened to cheerful music from _____ organ. Later, we had _____ picnic in the park. It was _____ exciting day!

## Lesson 1.9 Statements and Commands

A **statement** is a sentence that begins with a capital letter and ends with a period. A statement gives information.

**D**iego will be 13 in April.          **S**udan is a country in Africa.

**Commands** are sentences that tell you to do something. Commands also begin with a capital letter and end with a period.

**U**se the bright blue marker.          **C**hop the onions.

| Tip | Statements usually begin with a noun or a pronoun. Commands often begin with a verb. |
| --- | --- |

### Complete It

The statements below are missing periods. Add periods where they are needed. Circle each period you add so that it is easy to see.

Monday, July 16

Dear Diary,

On Saturday, Shi-Ann and I set up a lemonade stand  We made colorful signs to hang around the neighborhood  Dad helped us make cookies and chocolate pretzels  We wanted to make sure our customers would be thirsty

At the store, we bought a tablecloth, cups, and napkins  Dad let us borrow some money to use in our change box  Once we opened for business, we had tons of customers  Shi-Ann and I had to keep making fresh lemonade all day

We each made ten dollars from our lemonade stand  I had fun, but now I know that owning a business is a lot of work

## Lesson 1.9  Statements and Commands

### Identify It

Read the sentences below. If a sentence is a statement, write **S** in the space. If it is a command, write **C** in the space.

1. It is simple and fun to make your own lemonade. _____

2. Ask an adult to cut ten lemons in half. _____

3. Use a juicer to squeeze the juice from the lemons. _____

4. Mix the lemon juice with six cups of water. _____

5. The amount of sugar you add depends on how sweet you like your lemonade. _____

6. I use one cup of sugar. _____

7. Stir in the sugar until it dissolves. _____

8. Add some ice, and enjoy a glass of cool, refreshing lemonade. _____

### Try It

1. Write a command you might use to advertise a lemonade stand. Remember, a command usually begins with a verb.

   Example: Buy some cold, sweet lemonade today.

   _____

2. Write a statement about a business that you could start on your own.

   _____

# Lesson 1.10 Questions

**Questions** are sentences that ask something. When a person asks a question, he or she is looking for information. A question begins with a capital letter and ends with a question mark.

**W**ill you go to the party with me**?**

**W**hat is the weather like in Phoenix**?**

**Rewrite It**

Read each statement below. Then, rewrite it as a question.

Example: It was cold and rainy on Saturday.

<u>**What was the weather like on Saturday?**</u>

**1.** The largest frog in the world is called the Goliath frog.

_____

**2.** The skin of a toad feels dry and bumpy.

_____

**3.** Gliding leaf tree frogs can glide almost 50 feet in the air.

_____

**4.** The poison-dart frog lives in Colombia, South America.

_____

**5.** There are more than 4,000 species of frogs in the world.

_____

| Tip | Questions often begin with the words *who, what, where, when, how,* or *why.* |
|-----|-------------------------------------------------------------------------------|

# Lesson 1.10 Questions

## Proof It

Read the following paragraphs. There are seven incorrect end marks. Cross out the mistakes. Then, write the correct end marks above them.

Have you ever heard someone say it was "raining frogs". You might have thought that it was just a figure of speech. But in rare cases, it has actually rained frogs? How could this happen. It sounds impossible. During a tornado or a powerful thunderstorm, water from a pond or lake can be sucked into the air. This includes anything that is in the water.

The storm continues to move? As it travels, it releases the water into the air. Does this mean that frogs and fish come raining down from the sky. Yes, this is exactly what happens.

Cases of strange things falling from the sky have been reported for many years? People have seen small frogs, fish, grasshoppers, and snails drop from the sky in places like France, India, Louisiana, and Kansas. Are animals the only things that get swept up by storms. No. In fact, in 1995, it rained soda cans in the Midwest.

## Try It

1. Write a question you would like to ask a frog expert.

_____

2. Write a question you would like to ask a weather expert.

_____

## Lesson 1.11 Exclamations

**Exclamations** are sentences that show excitement or surprise. Exclamations begin with a capital letter and end with an exclamation point.

**T**he Gold Nuggets won the championship**!**

**W**e missed the bus**!**

Sometimes an exclamation can be a single word. Sometimes it can contain a command.

Oops!    Uh-oh!    Watch out!    Come back!

## Complete It

Read the advertisement below. Some of the end marks are missing. Write the correct end marks on the lines.

**Kirby's Toy Store** is closing.

Get new toys while they last___

Our store is open every night until 9:00___

We are located at the corner of Nelson Road and Ash Street___

Tell your friends___ Tell your neighbors___

Prices are being slashed every day! Toys are 50%-75% off___

**Don't miss out on the best toy sale of the year___**

## Lesson 1.11 Exclamations

**Proof It**

Read the sentences below. If the end mark is correct, make a check mark (✓) on the line. If the end mark is not correct, cross it out and write the correct end mark in the space.

1. Watch out. _____

2. Did you take the dog for a walk! _____

3. Luis is going to learn how to play the trumpet? _____

4. We won the game. _____

5. I lost my wallet? _____

6. How old is Ella. _____

7. My grandma had 16 brothers and sisters! _____

8. Harry wore a new suit to the wedding. _____

**Try It**

Imagine that you were going on a jungle animal safari. Think of two exclamations you might make. Write them on the lines below.
Examples: Watch out for that big snake!
          That leopard runs really fast!

_____

_____

## Review    Sentence Types

All sentences begin with a capital letter and end with a punctuation mark.

**Statements** are sentences that give information. A statement ends with a period.

> About 3,000 languages are spoken in the world today.

**Commands** are sentences that tell you to do something. A command usually begins with a verb and ends with a period.

> Put away the games when you have finished playing.

**Questions** are sentences that request, or ask, for information. A question ends with a question mark.

> When will Mr. Belzer arrive?

**Exclamations** are sentences that show surprise or excitement. An exclamation ends with an exclamation point.

> I can't wait to meet the star of the show!

**Putting It Together**

Read the sentences below. Add the correct end mark. Then, write **S** if the sentence is a statement, **Q** if it is a question, **E** if it is an exclamation, or **C** if it is a command.

1. Have you ever heard of the Guinness World Records__  _____

2. My sister tried to break the record for fastest backwards speller__  _____

3. Robert Wadlow, the tallest man, was 8 feet 11 inches tall__  _____

4. A dog named Olive Oyl set the record for jumping rope__  _____

5. What kind of evidence do you need to show that you have broken a record__  _____

6. Susan Williams blew a bubble larger than a basketball__  _____

7. Practice hard, and you may set a record one day __  _____

## Review   Sentence Types

Read the newspaper article below. There are eight mistakes in end punctuation. Cross out the incorrect end marks, and add the correct ones.

# Flying Fossett Sets Another Record

Steve Fossett is an interesting person who loves adventure! He has set many records. For example, in 1997, he flew around the world in a hot air balloon? In March of 2005, Steve broke another record. He flew solo around the world in an airplane without stopping. This flight took him more than 67 hours? Can you imagine sitting in a plane for that long.

Steve's plane weighed about 22,000 pounds. More than 18,000 pounds of the weight was fuel? Steve needed to be sure there would be enough fuel for the trip! For a while, it looked as though he might not have enough fuel. But Steve kept going and safely landed in Kansas. What an amazing trip. What record do you think Steve Fossett will set next.

1. Answer the following question with a statement: Why do you think Steve Fossett has set so many records?

   _____

2. If you could ask Steve one question, what would it be?

   _____

3. Imagine that you were there when Steve finished his flight. Think of an exclamation you might say to him. Write it on the line.

   _____

# Lesson 1.12 Parts of a Sentence: Subject

The **subject** of a sentence is what a sentence is about. In a statement, the subject is usually found at the beginning of the sentence before the verb. A subject can be a single word or it can be several words.

*The entire team* cheered when the winning goal was scored.

*Irina* loves to eat oatmeal for breakfast.

*Brian Adams and Brian Rowley* are in the same class.

*Four raccoons, three chipmunks, and an opossum* live in my backyard.

## Identify It

Underline the subject in each sentence below.

1. The Golden Gate Bridge is located in San Francisco, California.

2. The bridge was built in 1937.

3. It was the longest suspension bridge in the world until 1964.

4. A suspension bridge is a bridge that hangs from cables.

5. Joseph Strauss was the engineer who designed the amazing bridge.

6. The Verrazano Narrows Bridge and the Mackinac Bridge are two other famous bridges.

7. The bridge's orange color was chosen so that it would be easy to see on foggy days.

8. Many movies and TV shows have included views of the bridge.

9. You can walk or bike across the Golden Gate Bridge during the day.

## Lesson 1.12 Parts of a Sentence: Subject

**Complete It**

Each sentence below is missing a subject. Find the subject in the box that best fits each sentence. Write the subject on the line.

| The Golden Gate Bridge | A statue of Joseph B. Strauss |
| People and cars | Maria |
| The cost to build the bridge | About nine million people |

1. _____ learned all about different kinds of bridges from her teacher.

2. _____ is 1.7 miles long.

3. _____ celebrates the famous engineer.

4. _____ visit the bridge every year.

5. _____ that travel north on the bridge do not have to pay a toll.

6. _____ was 27 million dollars.

**Try It**

1. Write a sentence in which the subject is a person's name. Underline the subject.

_____

2. Write a sentence in which the subject is more than one word. Underline the subject.

_____

# Lesson 1.13 Parts of a Sentence: Predicate

A **predicate** tells what happens in a sentence. It tells what the subject is or does. The predicate always includes the verb. Finding the verb in a sentence can help you identify the predicate.

In the sentences below, the verbs are in bold type. The predicates are in italics.

> Evelina **recycles** *all her cans and bottles.*
> The seagull **soared** *above the stormy waters.*
> Jermaine **took** *a picture of the dog with his camera.*

## Identify It

Read the paragraph below. Underline the predicate in each sentence.

In the United States, April 22 is Earth Day. On Earth Day, people celebrate the planet Earth. They take the time to remember that the environment is fragile. The first Earth Day was held in 1970. About 20 million Americans celebrated that year. Today, more than 500 million people around the world take part in Earth Day activities.

On Earth Day, people learn about different types of pollution. They also learn what they can do to help save the planet. Many people recycle things. Paper, glass, and aluminum can be reused in new ways. Some groups plant trees to help keep the air clean. Others pick up litter in their parks and neighborhoods. For some caring people, every day is Earth Day!

## Lesson 1.13 Parts of a Sentence: Predicate

**Rewrite It**

One box below is filled with subjects. One box is filled with predicates. Draw a line to match each subject to a predicate. Then, write the complete sentences on the lines below. (There is more than one correct way to match the subjects and predicates.)

| Subjects | Predicates |
| --- | --- |
| Roma and Patrick | held an Earth Day 5K Run. |
| Alexis | cleaned up litter at McCoy Park. |
| Ms. Piazza's class | learned many ways to reuse newspapers. |
| My sister and I | donated ten dollars to a fund for endangered animals. |
| The students at Waxhill Elementary | planted eight small trees on Earth Day. |

1. _____

2. _____

3. _____

4. _____

5. _____

**Try It**

Write two sentences about something you can do every day to protect the planet. Underline the predicate in each sentence.

_____

_____

# Lesson 1.14 Sentence Fragments and Run-On Sentences

A sentence is a group of words that contains a complete thought or idea. All sentences have a subject and a predicate. Part of a sentence, or an incomplete sentence, is called a **sentence fragment**. Sentence fragments cannot stand alone.

Examples:  *Drove to the store.* (no subject)
*Because the sun.* (group of words)
*The girls on the porch.* (no predicate)

**Run-on sentences** are sentences that are too long. They are hard to follow, so they need to be split into two separate sentences. If the two sentences are about the same idea, they can be joined with a comma and a conjunction like *and* or *but*.

Clare likes cheese her brother Miles does not. (run-on)
Clare likes cheese. *Her* brother Miles does not. (split into two sentences)
Clare likes cheese, *but* her brother Miles does not. (combined with a comma and conjunction)

## Identify It

Read each item below. If it is a complete sentence, write **C** on the line. If it is a sentence fragment, write **F** on the line.

1. _____ Threw the ball.

2. _____ After Madeline made a basket.

3. _____ James scored a goal.

4. _____ Cheered, clapped, and yelled.

5. _____ The volleyball bounced off the net.

## Lesson 1.14 Sentence Fragments and Run-On Sentences

**Proof It**

Read the paragraphs below. There are four run-on sentences. Make a slash (/) where you would break the run-on sentences into two sentences.

Example: The clown wore enormous shoes / he had a large, red nose.

There are many different breeds of dogs each one has a special personality. Basset hounds are often thought of as hunting dogs. They have long, floppy ears and wrinkly skin they can be loyal, friendly, and stubborn. Some people think their droopy eyes are sweet others think these hounds always look sad.

Cocker spaniels are good dogs for families. They are friendly and good with children they have beautiful, long silky ears. Cocker spaniels are usually tan or black in color.

**Try It**

On a separate piece of paper, write two sentence fragments. Trade papers with a classmate. On the lines below, turn your classmate's fragments into complete sentences.

1. _____

2. _____

# Review   Parts of a Sentence, Sentence Fragments, and Run-On Sentences

The **subject** of a sentence tells who or what a sentence is about. A subject can be a single word, or it can be several words.

> *Simon* bought butter and eggs.
> *The green jacket and the dark gray coat* are too big for me.

A **predicate** tells what the subject is or does. The predicate in a sentence always includes the verb.

> The giant turtle *lay its eggs in the sand.*
> The mountains *look blue on rainy days.*

A **sentence fragment** is an incomplete sentence. Words need to be added to make a fragment a complete sentence.

> Locked the door. (fragment)
> Jamie locked the door. (sentence)

**Run-on sentences** are sentences that are too long. They can be split into two separate sentences, or they can be joined with a comma and a conjunction like *and* or *but.*

> Meg lives in the country *she* loves horses.
> Meg lives in the country. She loves horses.
> Meg lives in the country, *and* she loves horses.

## Putting It Together

In each sentence below, underline the subject and circle the predicate.

1. Early American farmers had many problems with their crops.

2. Insects, diseases, and bad weather ruined many crops.

3. Crows ate seeds and seedlings from the fields.

4. Farmers invented scarecrows to keep birds away from their plants.

5. Native Americans used a form of scarecrow to protect their fields, too.

# Review | Parts of a Sentence, Sentence Fragments, and Run-On Sentences

Read each item below. If it is a fragment, write **F** on the line. If it is a run-on sentence, write **RO** on the line. If it is a complete sentence, write **C** on the line. Then, underline the subject, and circle the predicate.

1. _____ Scarecrows did not scare birds away for long.

2. _____ Farmers had to.

3. _____ They used two poles for the body they stuffed the clothes with hay or leaves.

4. _____ Painted faces on the scarecrows' heads.

5. _____ Men's clothes were usually used women's clothes were often saved for other uses.

6. _____ The best scarecrows wore bells or other objects that made noise.

Read each run-on sentence below. If it should be split into two separate sentences, make a slash (/) in between the sentences. If the sentences are part of the same idea, add a comma and the word *and* or *but*. Use this symbol (^) to add a comma and the word.

**, but**
Example: George rode his bike ^ Stephanie walked.

1. Enzo and Shelley made their own scarecrow they named him Franklin.

2. They used Enzo's old overalls Shelley's dad gave them a straw hat.

3. Shelley and Enzo planned to use an old mop for the body they could not find one.

4. Enzo's mom donated a flowerpot Shelley and Enzo painted a face on it.

5. They put the scarecrow in the garden it scared away birds for a few days.

# Lesson 1.15 Combining Sentences: Subjects and Objects

Sometimes sentences that tell about the same thing can be combined. Then, the writer does not have to repeat words. Instead, the writer can combine two sentences into one by using the word *and*.

Terrence likes popcorn.          Peter likes popcorn.

Terrence *and* Peter like popcorn.

Because the subject (Terrence and Peter) is plural, the verb form has to change from *likes* to *like*.

In the example below, both sentences tell about what Jill read, so they can be combined.

Jill read a new book.          Jill read a magazine.

Jill read a new book *and* a magazine.

## Identify It

Read each pair of sentences below. If the sentences tell about the same thing and can be combined with the word *and*, make a check mark (✓) on the line. If they tell about different things and cannot be combined, make an **X** on the line.

1. _____ Snakes are reptiles. Lizards are reptiles.

2. _____ Cheetahs are mammals. Toads are amphibians.

3. _____ The robin ate some berries. The robin ate a worm.

4. _____ Tarantulas are spiders. Black widows are spiders.

5. _____ The dolphin swam beside its baby. The whale headed for deeper waters.

## Lesson 1.15 Combining Sentences: Subjects and Objects

**Rewrite It**

Combine each pair of sentences below into one sentence. Write the new sentence on the line.

1. Bobcats live in the mountains of Virginia.
   Bears live in the mountains of Virginia.

   _____

2. The deer drinks from the stream. The coyote drinks from the stream.

   _____

3. The airplane startled the rabbit. The airplane startled the owl.

   _____

4. It is rare to spot mountain lions. It is rare to spot bald eagles.

   _____

5. Andy saw a deer at dusk. Andy saw a raccoon at dusk.

   _____

**Try It**

Write two sentences about wild animals you have seen. Then, combine your sentences into a single sentence.

Example:  I saw a wild turkey. I saw a woodpecker.
          I saw a wild turkey and a woodpecker.

_____

_____

_____

_____

## Lesson 1.16 Combining Sentences: Verbs

When two sentences tell about the same thing, they can sometimes be combined using the word *and*. The first two sentences below are about what Veronica did at breakfast, so they can be combined.

> Veronica ate some cereal. Veronica drank a glass of orange juice.
>
> Veronica ate some cereal *and* drank a glass of orange juice.

Some sentences can be combined using the word *or*. Use *or* if there are several choices about what might happen. In the example below, we do not know which choice Habib will make, so the word *or* is used.

> Habib might walk home. Habib might ride his bike home. Habib might run home.
>
> Habib might walk, ride his bike, *or* run home.

If you list several things in a row, place a comma after each one.

### Complete It

Read the sentences below. Fill in each blank with the missing word.

1. Grandpa spread out the tent. Grandpa hammered the stakes.

   Grandpa spread out the tent _____ hammered the stakes.

2. Will might look for sticks. Will might cook dinner.

   Will might look for sticks _____ cook dinner.

3. Will put the pillows in the tent. Will unrolled the sleeping bags.

   Will put the pillows in the tent _____ unrolled the sleeping bags.

4. Grandpa and Will might make sandwiches. Grandpa and Will might grill hamburgers.

   Grandpa and Will might make sandwiches _____ grill hamburgers.

# Lesson 1.16 Combining Sentences: Verbs

**Rewrite It**

Combine each set of sentences below into one
sentence. Write the new sentence on the line.

1. Grandpa stacked the wood. Grandpa
found the matches. Grandpa lit the fire.

_____

2. Grandpa toasted a marshmallow. Grandpa placed it between two
graham crackers.

_____

3. Will read in the tent with a flashlight. Will finished his book.

_____

4. Grandpa and Will looked at the night sky. Grandpa and Will found the
Big Dipper.

_____

5. Next summer, they might sail down the coast. Next summer, they might
go fishing.

_____

**Try It**

1. Write two sentences that tell about things you do in the morning. Use a
different verb in each sentence.

_____

_____

2. Now, combine the two sentences you wrote using the word *and*.

_____

# Lesson 1.17 Combining Sentences: Adjectives

Sometimes, sentences can be combined.

The leaves are green. They are shiny. They are large.

The adjectives *green*, *shiny*, and *large* all describe *leaves*. The sentences can be combined into one by using the word *and*. Remember to use a comma after each adjective except the last.

The leaves are green, shiny, *and* large.

In the example below, only a comma is needed to combine the two sentences. Both sentences describe the jacket.

The red jacket is Amelia's favorite. The jacket is warm.

The warm, red jacket is Amelia's favorite.

**Identify It**

Read each set of sentences below. If the adjectives describe the same thing, the sentences can be combined. Make a check mark (✓) on the line. If they describe different things, the sentences cannot be combined. Make an **X** on the line.

1. _____ The strawberries are red. They are juicy.

2. _____ The lemons are tart. The lemonade is sweet.

3. _____ I like wild blueberries. I like fresh blueberries.

4. _____ The grapes are ripe. They are dark purple. They are plump.

5. _____ The fuzzy kiwi is on the table. It is round.

6. _____ Oranges are tropical. Apples can be red, green, or yellow.

## Lesson 1.17 Combining Sentences: Adjectives

**Rewrite It**

Combine each set of sentences below into one sentence. Write the new sentence on the line.

1. Cucumbers are long. They are thin. They are green.

   _____

2. Sam grew some huge tomatoes in his garden. They were juicy.

   _____

3. The rabbits seem to love Mom's lettuce. It is leafy.

   _____

4. The seedlings are tiny. The seedlings are pale green.

   _____

5. Rohan's peppers were small. They were spicy.

   _____

**Try It**

1. Write two sentences that describe a piece of clothing you are wearing. Use a different adjective in each sentence.

   Example: I am wearing a new shirt. My shirt is striped.

   _____

   _____

2. Now, write a sentence that combines the two sentences you wrote.

   Example: I am wearing a new, striped shirt.

   _____

## Review | Combining Sentences

When sentences tell about the same thing, they can be combined. This helps the writer avoid repeating words. Commas and the words *and* and *or* are often used to combine sentences.

> Kirsten lives in San Diego.          Rafael lives in San Diego.
> Kirsten *and* Rafael live in San Diego.

> Bianca might take piano lessons.     Bianca might join a club.
> Bianca might take piano lessons *or* join a club.

> The popcorn is hot.   It is salty.   It is tasty.
> The hot, salty popcorn is tasty.   OR   The popcorn is hot, salty, *and* tasty.

**Putting It Together**

Read the sentences below. Fill in each blank with a comma or the missing word or words.

**I.** The Tangs went to the Mojave Desert. They went to Las Vegas. They went to Kelso Dunes.

_____ went to the Mojave Desert _____ Las Vegas, and Kelso Dunes.

**2.** The San Gabriel Mountains border the Mojave. The San Bernadino Mountains border the Mojave.

The San Gabriel Mountains _____ the San Bernadino Mountains _____ the Mojave.

**3.** The world's largest thermometer is 135 feet tall. The thermometer is located in the Mojave.

_____ is 135 feet tall _____ is located in the Mojave.

## Review  Combining Sentences

Combine each set of sentences below into one sentence. Write the new sentence on the line.

1. Joshua trees live in the Mojave Desert. Joshua trees grow slowly.

   _____

2. Joshua trees are found in California and Arizona. They are found in Utah. They are found in Nevada.

   _____

3. Native Americans made rope from the Mojave yucca plant. They made sandals and cloth from the Mojave yucca plant.

   _____

4. July is very hot in the Mojave Desert. August is very hot in the Mojave Desert.

   _____

5. The kit fox lives in deserts, on prairies, and on plains. The kit fox is small. It is gray.

   _____

6. The kit fox hunts at night. It eats small mammals.

   _____

7. Desert tortoises spend most of their lives underground. They can live for a year without water.

   _____

8. Desert tortoises eat grasses. They eat wildflowers.

   _____

The first word of a sentence always begins with a **capital letter**. A capital letter is a sign to the reader that a new sentence is starting.

*I* live on the third floor of the apartment building.

*Do* you like green beans?

*Here* comes the parade!

*Maya* grinned at Jeff.

**Proof It**

Read the paragraphs below. The first word of every sentence should be capitalized. To capitalize a letter, underline it three times (≡). Then, write the capital letter above it.

Example: <u>m</u>y sister taught me a new computer game.

have you ever played golf? if you have, you know that it can be harder than it looks. golfer Michelle Wie makes it look pretty easy. that's because she can hit a golf ball more than 300 yards! at the age of 13, Michelle became the youngest winner ever of the Women's Amateur Public Links. she has even played on the famous men's golf tour, the PGA Tour. some people think that this amazing six-foot-tall golfer will be the next Tiger Woods.

## Lesson 2.1 Capitalizing the First Word in a Sentence

**Rewrite It**

Rewrite each sentence below. Make sure your sentences begin with a capital letter.

1. michelle Wie's family is Korean.

   _____

2. she started beating her parents at golf when she was about eight.

   _____

3. today, Michelle plays regularly on the LPGA Tour.

   _____

4. *competitive* and *determined* are two words that describe Michelle.

   _____

5. david Leadbetter was Michelle's coach for years.

   _____

6. what kind of golfing records will Michelle set in the future?

   _____

**Try It**

1. What sports do you like to play or watch? Begin your sentence with a capital letter.

   _____

2. What sports figure do you most admire? Begin your sentence with a capital letter.

   _____

## Lesson 2.2   Capitalizing Names and Titles

Capitalize the **specific names of people and pets**.

My cousin *Umeko* moved here from Japan.
We named the puppy *George*.

A **title** is a word that comes before a person's name. A title gives more information about who a person is. Titles that come before a name are capitalized.

| | |
|---|---|
| *Grandpa* Bruce | *Aunt* Juliet |
| *Captain* Albrecht | *President* Abraham Lincoln |
| *Senator* Barbara Boxer | *Judge* Naser |

**Titles of respect** are also capitalized.

| | | |
|---|---|---|
| *Mr.* Watterson | *Miss* Newton | *Mrs.* Cohen |
| *Dr.* Gupta | *Ms.* Liang | |

| Tip | If a title is not used with a name, it is not capitalized.<br>My *aunt* is funny. The *judge* was here.<br>But, if a title is used as a name, it is capitalized.<br>Tell *Mom* I am going to the park.<br>*Grandpa* will fix the computer. |
|---|---|

**Complete It**

Complete each sentence below with the words in parentheses ( ). Some of the words will need to be capitalized. Others will not.

1. Kelly took her dog, _____, for a walk to the park. (abby)

2. My school has a new _____. (principal)

3. On Tuesday, _____ is coming to visit. (grandma)

4. The best teacher I ever had was _____. (mr. butler)

5. The baby dolphin at the zoo is named _____. (michi)

## Lesson 2.2 Capitalizing Names and Titles

**Proof It**

Read the letter below. There are ten mistakes. To capitalize a letter, underline it three times, and write the capital letter above it. To lowercase a letter (or change it from a capital letter to a small letter), make a slash through it. Then, write the small letter above it.

Example: Olivia and <u>m</u>att asked their Grandma if she knew <u>m</u>r. Buckman.

April 12

Dear mayor Hendricks,

My name is annie Chun. My aunt and Uncle live near Pebblebrook Creek. When I visited them last week, we went wading. We were looking for rocks for a science project I am doing in mrs. sutton's class. We found the rocks, but we found many other things, too. For example, aunt Rose found several soda cans. Uncle Richard found some candy wrappers. Their dog, louie, discovered an old bottle. He thought it was a bone.

I would like to organize a cleanup of Pebblebrook Creek. I know the environment is important to you as the town Mayor. Can you help me organize this event? Maybe the next time my Aunt, uncle, Louie, and I go wading, we won't find anything but rocks.

Sincerely,

Annie chun

## Lesson 2.3  Capitalizing Place Names

The **names of specific places** always begin with a capital letter.

| | |
|---|---|
| *Madison, Wisconsin* | *Rocky Mountains* |
| *Italy* | *Liberty Avenue* |
| *Science Museum of Minnesota* | *Jupiter* |
| *Jones Middle School* | *Los Angeles Public Library* |

**Complete It**

Complete each sentence below with the word or words in parentheses ( ).
Remember to capitalize the names of specific places.

1. There are many _____ (towns) across _____ (america) that have interesting names.

2. Have you ever heard of Okay, _____ (arkansas)?

3. Some towns are named after foods, like Avocado, California, and _____ (two egg), Florida.

4. Some names, like Chickasawhatchee and _____ (goochland) are fun to say.

5. A person from _____ (russia) might be surprised to find a town named Moscow in Vermont.

6. If you're on your way to visit _____ (mount rushmore), look for Igloo, South Dakota.

7. Would you like to go to _____ (boring elementary school) in Boring, Oregon?

| Tip | In the names of specific places, some words are not capitalized. All the important words begin with a capital letter. Small words, like *of*, *the*, *and*, and *a*, do not begin with a capital letter unless they are at the beginning of a sentence. |
|---|---|

## Lesson 2.3  Capitalizing Place Names

**Proof It**

Read the directions below. Capitalize the names of specific places. To capitalize a letter, underline it three times (≡), and write the capital letter above it.

- Take wilbur street to preston parkway, and turn left.

- Travel about two miles on preston parkway.

- You will pass montgomery library and the talbot recreation center.

- At the light, turn right onto solomon road.

- You will drive over haystack bridge and pass a gas station.

- children's playhouse is located on the west side of the street.

- The address is 1548 solomon road.

**Try It**

On the lines below, write your own set of directions from your home to a friend's house. Be sure to include street names and any landmarks like schools, libraries, parks, and so on.

_____

_____

_____

_____

_____

# Lesson 2.4    Capitalizing Dates and Holidays

The **days of the week** each begin with a capital letter.

Monday, Tuesday, Wednesday, Thursday, Friday, Saturday, Sunday

The **months of the year** are capitalized.

January, February, March, April, May, June, July,
August, September, October, November, December

The **names of holidays** are capitalized.

Memorial Day, Mother's Day,
Thanksgiving, Kwanzaa

## Complete It

Complete the sentences below with the name of a day, month, or holiday. Remember to use capital letters where needed.

1. I was born in the month of _____.

2. On _____, many people stay up until midnight to welcome the new year.

3. My favorite day of the week is _____.

4. On _____, Austin made a card for his dad and washed his dad's car.

5. _____ is the middle of the week.

6. In northern states, it often snows in _____.

7. The groundhog did not see his shadow on _____ this year.

8. Independence Day is on _____ 4th every year.

> **Tip** The names of the seasons (*spring, summer, autumn,* and *winter*) are not capitalized unless they appear at the beginning of a sentence.

## Lesson 2.4  Capitalizing Dates and Holidays

**Rewrite It**

Rewrite the sentences below. Capitalize the names of days, months, and holidays.

1. presidents' day is on monday, february 21.

_____

2. If the weather is nice, we will have a cookout on labor day.

_____

3. thanksgiving day always falls on a thursday.

_____

4. Ty gave a valentine to every person in his class on valentine's day.

_____

5. Jessy is having a pool party on saturday, june 20.

_____

**Try It**

1. What is your favorite holiday? Why?

_____

_____

2. What is the coldest month of the year where you live? What is the warmest month?

_____

_____

## Lesson 2.5   Capitalizing Book, Movie, and Song Titles

The titles of books, movies, and songs are capitalized. Small words, like *of*, *the*, *and*, *in*, *to*, *a*, *an*, and *from*, do not begin with a capital letter unless they are the first or last word of a title.

| Books | Movies | Songs |
|---|---|---|
| Stuart Little | Epic | "Down by the Bay" |
| Ramona the Brave | The Secret Garden | "Pop Goes the Weasel" |
| A Light in the Attic | Jumanji | "When You Wish Upon a Star" |

**Rewrite It**

Rewrite the sentences below. Capitalize the names of books, movies, and song titles.

1. It took Shakhil only two days to read the book <u>how to eat fried worms</u>.

   _____

2. Sara is sleeping over tonight, and we are going to watch <u>toy story 2</u>.

   _____

3. The song "let it go" is from the movie frozen.

   _____

4. I love the poems in Bruce Lansky's book <u>no more homework, no more tests</u>.

   _____

5. Devon listened to the song "yellow submarine" on his mom's Beatles' CD.

   _____

## Lesson 2.5  Capitalizing Book, Movie, and Song Titles

**Proof It**

Read the sentences below. There are 24 words that should begin with a capital letter but do not. To capitalize a letter, underline it three times. Then, write the capital letter above it.

1. I love to sing "hakuna matata" from <u>the Lion King</u> because the words are fun to say.

2. Have you seen the old version or the new version of <u>The parent trap</u>?

3. Felipe borrowed <u>the way things work</u> by David Macaulay from the library.

4. If you watch <u>Schoolhouse Rock</u>, you can learn the song "conjunction junction."

5. Last week, Lottie read <u>Freckle juice</u> and <u>Chocolate fever</u>.

6. <u>madeline</u> is the name of a book and a movie.

7. Reading <u>the great kapok tree</u> by Lynne Cherry is a good way to learn about rain forests.

8. My little sister sings "shake your sillies out" every morning.

9. Paul and Tyler saw <u>walking with dinosaurs</u> three times in the movie theater!

**Try It**

1. Imagine that you were shipwrecked on a desert island. If you could bring only one book with you, what would it be?

_____

2. What is the funniest movie you have seen in the last year?

_____

## Review   Capitalization

All **sentences** begin with a capital letter.

Kangaroos, koalas, and opossums all have pouches.

Capitalize the **specific names of people and pets**.

Toddy and Brian have a puppy named Sweet Pea.

**Titles** that come before a name are capitalized.

Uncle Josh    Grandma Lea    Officer Romero

**Titles of respect** are also capitalized.

Miss Wyatt    Mr. Liang    Dr. Elliot

The **names of specific places** always begin with a capital letter.

Cartwright Avenue    Brazil    Alabama    Sampson High School

The **days of the week** each begin with a capital letter.

Monday    Wednesday    Thursday    Saturday

The **months of the year** are capitalized.

January    March    September    December

The **names of holidays** are capitalized.

Father's Day    Earth Day    Groundhog Day

The **titles of books, movies, and songs** are capitalized. Words like *of, the, and, in, to, a, an,* and *from* do not begin with a capital letter unless they are the first or last word of a title.

A Bug's Life    Aesop's Fables    "You Are My Sunshine"

## Review  Capitalization

**Putting It Together**

Read the paragraph below. Find the nine mistakes in capitalization. To capitalize a letter, underline it three times. Then, write the capital letter above it.

saturday, july 7 was Lily's birthday. Lily and Mom decided that a movie

marathon would be fun. Lily chose three movies to show at her party:

Finding nemo, Hook, and the princess bride. Mom made popcorn balls.

grandpa Henry made strawberry and chocolate ice-cream shakes. Lily

could not wait for her friends Gabe, Tamiko, eliza, and Ben to arrive. she

knew that her eighth birthday party was going to be a good one.

Complete each sentence below with the words in parentheses ( ). Some of the words will need to be capitalized. Others will not.

**1.** Tamiko's parents were born in _____. (japan)

**2.** Gabe's birthday is on _____. (new year's day)

**3.** Lily's friends sang _____ when she blew out her candles. ("happy birthday")

**4.** Lily's _____ was born in 1947. (grandma)

**5.** Gabe and Eliza bought a birthday present for Lily on _____. (thursday)

**6.** Lily loves to go to the _____ with her mom. (movies)

## Lesson 2.6   Periods

A **period** is an end mark that follows a statement or a command.

> Put your bike in the garage.        Natalie has four brothers.

Periods are also used after initials. An **initial** is a letter that stands for a name.

> Darren *B.* Johnson    *P. L.* Travers    *J. P.* O'Bryan

The **days of the week** are often written as abbreviations, or in a shorter form. A period follows the abbreviation.

> Mon.  Tues.  Wed.  Thurs.  Fri.  Sat.  Sun.

The **months of the year** can also be abbreviated. May, June, and July are not abbreviated because their names are short.

> Jan.  Feb.  Mar.  Apr.  Aug.  Sept.  Oct.  Nov.  Dec.

**People's titles** are usually abbreviated when they come before a name.

> *Mrs.* = mistress   *Mr.* = mister   *Dr.* = doctor

**Types of streets** are written as abbreviations in addresses.

> *St.* = street    *Ave.* = avenue     *Dr.* = drive    *Ln.* = lane
> *Rd.* = road     *Blvd.* = boulevard    *Ct.* = court    *Cir.* = circle

## Match It

Write the letter of the correct abbreviation on the line.

1. _____ October 2              **a.** Oct. 2          **b.** Octob. 2

2. _____ John Fitzgerald Kennedy  **a.** John F Kennedy  **b.** John F. Kennedy

3. _____ Tuesday             **a.** Tu.            **b.** Tues.

4. _____ Chester Avenue       **a.** Chester Avn.    **b.** Chester Ave.

5. _____ December 19          **a.** Dec. 19        **b.** Dcmbr. 19

6. _____ Madison Anne Hall     **a.** Madison A Hall   **b.** Madison A. Hall

## Lesson 2.6  Periods

**Proof It**

Read the schedule below. Cross out words that can be written as abbreviations. Write the correct abbreviations above them.

| | |
|---|---|
| Monday, March 7 | Hot Potatoes concert at 422 Lakeshore Drive—7:00 |
| Thursday, April 14 | Cassie's dentist appointment with Doctor Phillips—10:00 |
| Friday, April 29 | Meeting with Mister Haddad—noon |
| Saturday, May 21 | Drop-off costumes at Mistress Jensen's house—1668 Dublin Lane |
| Tuesday, August 30 | Jimmy Ortega's birthday party—46 Brentwood Boulevard |
| Sunday, September 18 | Brunch with Mister Sato—11:00 |

**Try It**

1. Write a sentence about what you would do if someone gave you a hundred-dollar bill. End your sentence with a period.

_____

2. Ask three friends when their birthdays are. Write the dates on the line using abbreviations for the names of the months.

_____

| Tip | Abbreviations for days, months, and types of streets are used only in addresses and casual writing. For example, you might abbreviate the name of a day or month in a calendar or a note. Do not use these abbreviations in the body of a letter, a report, or a story. |
|---|---|

# Lesson 2.7  Question Marks

Use a **question mark** to end a sentence that asks a question.

Would you like some fruit punch**?**   How many books did you read**?**
Where is Connor going**?**   Can all birds fly**?**

**Complete It**

Read each answer below. Then, write the question that goes with the answer.

Example: **Q:**  <u>How tall is Mr. Stein?</u>
        **A:** Mr. Stein is six feet tall.

1. **Q:** _____

    **A:** Jupiter has at least 63 known moons.

2. **Q:** _____

    **A:** The sun is the largest body in the solar system.

3. **Q:** _____

    **A:** Mars is closer to the sun than Saturn.

4. **Q:** _____

    **A:** Galileo made his first telescope in 1608.

5. **Q:** _____

    **A:** Astronaut Shannon Lucid has spent more than 200 days in space.

6. **Q:** _____

    **A:** Mercury is the smallest planet.

## Lesson 2.7　Question Marks

**Proof It**
Read the paragraphs below. Cross out the six incorrect end marks. Add the correct end marks, and circle them.

Have you ever visited the Sleeping Bear Dunes. They are located along the shore of Lake Michigan. The enormous dunes, or sand hills, are more than 400 feet tall in places. Many people travel to Michigan every year to climb the dunes? Most visitors come in the summer, but some people come in the winter, instead. Why would they visit the icy shores of the lake in the winter. Sledding down the steep slopes can be a lot of fun!

Do you know where the dunes got their name. A Native American legend says that a mother bear lay on the beach to watch for her cubs after a fire. Over time, sand covered the bear? Some people still think they can see the shape of a bear sleeping on the beach. This is how the dunes came to be called the Sleeping Bear Dunes?

**Try It**
On the lines below, write a question you could ask a park ranger at Sleeping Bear Dunes National Lakeshore.

_____

_____

## Lesson 2.8   Exclamation Points

An **exclamation point** is used to end a sentence that is exciting or expresses strong feeling. Sometimes exclamation points are used to show surprise or fear.

That pan is hot!                    Lindsay won first-prize!

I can't believe you broke the chair!    There's a snake!

**Proof It**

Read the diary entry below. Five of the periods should be exclamation points. Find the five incorrect periods, and cross them out. Then, add exclamation points where they are needed.

Saturday, May 6

Dear Diary,

    Something interesting happened today. I am going to be in a movie. The movie <u>The Time Travelers</u> is being filmed in my town. My mom works at the library. The director was learning about the history of the town at the library. My mom helped the director find what she needed. The director saw my picture on my mom's desk. She asked my mom if I would be interested in a small part in the movie. Would I ever.

    I will have only two lines to say. Mom said she will help me memorize them. My scene will last about five minutes. Do you know what the best part is? I get to work with my favorite actor. I can't wait to start filming. Who knows? Maybe I'll be famous one day.

## Lesson 2.8 Exclamation Points

### Complete It

The sentences below are missing end marks. Add the correct end mark in the space following each sentence. You should add four periods, two question marks, and three exclamation points.

1. Evan and Tanner have been jumping on the trampoline all morning___

2. Have you read the book <u>A Cricket in Times Square</u> ___

3. Kazuki's swimming lesson was cancelled___

4. Watch out___

5. Please clean your room before bedtime___

6. The Bradview Tigers won the championship___

7. Would you like cheese on your sandwich___

8. There's a huge spider in my bed___

9. Tereza traded stickers with her little brother___

### Try It

1. Write a sentence that shows excitement. Your sentence should end with an exclamation point.

   _____

2. Write a sentence that shows fear. Your sentence should end with an exclamation point.

   _____

## Review    End Marks and Abbreviations

A **period** is used at the end of a statement or a command.

Reggie has a spelling test.          Stir the batter until it is smooth.

An **initial** is a letter, followed by a period, that stands for a name.

James *K.* Polk    *A. L.* Wilhelm    Annette *P.* Desmond

The **days of the week** can be written as abbreviations.

Mon.  Tues.  Wed.  Thurs.  Fri.  Sat.  Sun.

The **months of the year** can also be written as abbreviations.

Jan.  Feb.  Mar.  Apr.  Aug.  Sept.  Oct.  Nov.  Dec.

**People's titles** are usually abbreviated when they come before a name.

*Mrs.* = mistress    *Mr.* = mister    *Dr.* = doctor

**Types of streets** are abbreviated in addresses.

*St.* = street    *Dr.* = drive    *Ln.* = lane    *Rd.* = road    *Ct.* = court

A **question mark** is used to end a sentence that asks a question.

Are you feeling better**?**          What do penguins eat**?**

An **exclamation point** is used to end a sentence that shows excitement, strong feeling, surprise, or fear.

My drawing won the contest**!**    Help**!**    This is the best party**!**

**Putting It Together**

Rewrite each item below using abbreviations wherever possible.

1. Saturday, November 4 _____

2. Doctor Khouri _____

3. 1452 Winding Wood Lane _____

4. Mistress Bryson _____

5. John Paul Garrison _____

## Review | End Marks and Abbreviations

Read the following paragraph. There are five incorrect end marks. Cross out the mistakes. Then, write the correct end marks above them.

When people go on vacation, they usually stay in a hotel or an inn. Some stay in cottages or cabins? Campers often sleep in tents! But have you ever heard of someone going on vacation and sleeping in a treehouse. If this sounds like fun, you might want to learn more about Out 'n' About Treesort. This unusual resort is located in Takilma, Oregon! There are 18 treehouses at Out 'n' About. There are also seven swinging bridges and five swings. Don't go there for a visit if you are afraid of heights.

Read the sentences below. If the end mark is correct, make a check mark (✓) in the space. If the end mark is not correct, cross it out and write the correct end mark on the line.

1. What kind of activities can kids do at Out 'n' About Treesort. _____

2. They can go horseback riding and rafting. _____

3. The highest part of the floating pirate ship is 52 feet from the ground? _____

4. Everyone is friends at the Treesort, and there are no locks on the doors! _____

5. Would your family enjoy sleeping in a treehouse? _____

## Lesson 2.9 Commas with Dates, Cities, States, and Addresses

Commas are used in dates. They are used in between the day and the year.

March 4, 2006    September 22, 1750    June 1, 1991

Commas are also used in between the names of cities and states or cities and countries.

Portland, Oregon    Paris, France    Minneapolis, Minnesota

When the names of cities and states (or countries) are in the middle of a sentence, a comma goes after the state or country, too.

Bethany stopped in Burlington, Vermont, on her way home.

In an address, a comma is used between the city name and state abbreviation.

Richmond, VA    Juneau, AK

**Proof It**

Read the sentences below. Add commas by using this symbol (∧).

Example: The Rock and Roll Hall of Fame is in Cleveland∧Ohio.

1. Basketball star LeBron James was born on December 30 1984.

2. Sarah Hughes skated in the Winter Olympics in Salt Lake City Utah.

3. In 2004, Lance Armstrong traveled to Liege Belgium to ride in the Tour de France.

4. Olympic swimmer Michael Phelps was born in Baltimore Maryland in 1985.

| Tip | When only a month and year are given, do not separate them with a comma. August 1999    February 2014    December 1941 |
|-----|---|

# Lesson 2.9 Commas with Dates, Cities, States, and Addresses

## Identify It

There are two choices below for each item. Choose the correct version, and write the letter in the space.

1. _____ **a.** October, 12 1954    **b.** October 12, 1954

2. _____ **a.** Omaha, NE    **b.** Omaha NE

3. _____ **a.** August, 2007    **b.** August 2007

4. _____ **a.** January 24, 1936    **b.** January, 24, 1936

5. _____ **a.** Amarillo Texas    **b.** Amarillo, Texas

6. _____ **a.** September 30, 2015    **b.** September 30 2015,

7. _____ **a.** Nashville, Tennessee, is 284 miles from Shreveport, Louisiana.
       **b.** Nashville Tennessee, is 284 miles from Shreveport, Louisiana.

8. _____ **a.** The ship traveled from Crete, Greece, to the shores of Turkey.
       **b.** The ship traveled from Crete, Greece to the shores of Turkey.

## Try It

Ask two people in your class or your family the questions below. Record their answers on the lines.

1. In what city and state were you born?

_____

_____

2. What is your birth date?

_____

_____

# Lesson 2.10 Commas in a Series

A **series** is a list of words. Use a comma after each word in a series except the last word.

> Ms. Pinckney asked Alonzo, Erica, and Charley to work on the project together.
> Dakota put a sandwich, an apple, and a granola bar in her lunchbox.
> Our neighbors have two dogs, three cats, seven chickens, and a goat.

## Proof It

Read the note below. Twelve commas are missing. Add commas where they are needed by using this symbol (∧).

---

Dear Dillon,

Please go to the store for me when you get home from school. Tonight we are going to make muffins for Grandad's birthday breakfast. We will need blueberries eggs sugar and lemon juice. I left some money on the kitchen table.

Ellie is going swimming with Rob Aliya Eve and Hunter. She will be home around 4:00. Please remind her to let the dog out hang up her swimsuit and start her homework.

I made a list of the things you said you will need for your science project. I put glue sand newspaper vinegar and baking soda on the list. Is anything missing? We can go shopping tomorrow afternoon.

See you in a couple of hours!

Love,

Mom

---

## Lesson 2.10 Commas in a Series

**Rewrite It**

The numbered sentences are missing commas. Rewrite each numbered sentence in the recipe, using commas where needed.

### Lemony Blueberry Muffins

1½ cups flour
½ cup yellow cornmeal
½ cup sugar
1½ teaspoons baking powder
½ teaspoon baking soda
¼ teaspoon salt

½ cup milk
½ cup plain yogurt
3 tablespoons oil
1 tablespoon lemon juice
1 egg
1 cup blueberries

*Always have an adult help you when you are cooking.

- (1) You will also need cooking spray a muffin tin a measuring cup two bowls a teaspoon a tablespoon and a wooden spoon.

_____

_____

- Preheat the oven to 400°F. Spoon the flour into the measuring cup.
- (2) Combine the flour cornmeal sugar baking powder baking soda and salt.

_____

- (3) In the other bowl, combine the milk yogurt oil lemon juice and egg.

_____

- Add the wet mixture to the flour mixture. Stir until moist. Fold in the blueberries.
- Spoon the batter into the muffin tin. Bake at 400°F for 20 minutes.
- (4) Remove the muffins from the pan place them on a wire rack and let them cool.

_____

## Lesson 2.11 Commas in Compound Sentences

A **simple sentence** tells about one complete thought. A **compound sentence** is made of two or more simple sentences. To form a compound sentence, use a comma and the conjunction *and, or,* or *but* to join the simple sentences.

In the examples below, the underlined parts of each compound sentence can stand alone as simple sentences. Notice that a comma follows the first simple sentence.

<u>Sadie likes orange juice</u>, *but* <u>her brother prefers apple juice.</u>
<u>Do you want to go to the zoo</u>, *or* <u>would you rather go to the art museum?</u>
<u>Alejandro collects baseball cards</u>, *and* <u>Adam collects coins.</u>

**Identify It**

Read each sentence below. If it is a simple sentence, write **S** on the line. If it is a compound sentence, write **C** on the line. Then, underline each simple sentence in the compound sentence.

1. _____ Have you noticed birds in your yard or your neighborhood?

2. _____ Feeding birds can be fun, and it can be educational.

3. _____ Some birds like birdseed, but others like suet, a type of fat.

4. _____ In the winter, many birds prefer fatty foods, like peanut butter.

5. _____ Bird food placed on the ground will attract birds, but it will also attract other animals.

6. _____ Squirrels are known for eating bird food and scaring birds away.

7. _____ Once birds notice that you are feeding them, they will come to visit often.

8. _____ Finches love thistle seed, and orioles love oranges.

## Lesson 2.11 Commas in Compound Sentences

**Proof It**

Read the paragraph below. Three commas are missing from compound sentences. Add each comma by using this symbol (∧).

If you have a plastic soda bottle, you can make your own bird feeder. With an adult's help, make two holes on opposite sides of the bottle and push a twig through each hole. Small birds can perch on the twig. Then, make several other holes in the bottle. The birds will be able to eat seeds from these holes. Tie some string around the neck of the bottle and hang it from a sturdy tree branch. Enjoy watching the birds from a window but don't forget to feed them.

**Try It**

1. Write a simple sentence about birds you have seen at a park or in your neighborhood.

_____

_____

2. Write a compound sentence about other city wildlife you have seen.

_____

_____

## Review   Comma Usage

In dates, commas are placed in between the day of the month and the year. Do not use a comma between a month and a year.

November 1, 1957    April 4, 2005    May 29, 1998    July 2000

**Commas** are also placed in between the names of cities and states or countries. When these names are in the middle of a sentence, a comma goes after the name of the state or country, too. In an address, a comma goes between the city name and state abbreviation.

Wichita, Kansas    Syracuse, NY    London, England

Takumi moved from Baltimore, Maryland, to Eugene, Oregon.

Place a comma after each word in a **series** except the last word.

The soccer ball, football, and basketball are in the garage.

A **compound sentence** is made of two or more simple sentences joined with a comma and the word *and*, *or*, or *but*.

Carla wanted to go to a movie, *but* Scott wanted to stay home.

**Putting It Together**

Read the paragraph below. It is missing seven commas. Add the commas where they are needed using this symbol (∧).

On May 14 1804, a group of explorers left Saint Charles Missouri.

Thomas Jefferson had hired Meriwether Lewis and William Clark to explore

the American West. Jefferson wanted the group to learn about the land

the animals the plants and Native American tribes. The group followed

the Missouri River west. They spent their first winter near a town that today

is called Washburn North Dakota. A Native American woman named

Sacagawea joined the group in November 1804. She was a helpful guide

but her greatest skill was as a translator.

## Review  Comma Usage

Rewrite each sentence below. Add commas where they are needed.

**1.** Lewis and Clark met native people from the Oto the Blackfeet and the Sioux tribes.

_____

_____

**2.** Jefferson hoped they would find water that connected the oceans but they did not.

_____

_____

**3.** Hunters soldiers and boatmen made up much of Lewis and Clark's group of explorers.

_____

_____

**4.** The group returned to St. Louis Missouri on September 23 1806.

_____

_____

There are two choices below for each item. Choose the correct version, and write the letter on the line.

**1.** _____ **a.** August 1804          **b.** August, 1804

**2.** _____ **a.** November 4, 1804     **b.** November, 4 1804

**3.** _____ **a.** Portland ME          **b.** Portland, ME

# Lesson 2.12 Punctuating Dialogue

The exact words a person says are called **dialogue**. One set of quotation marks is used before the first word of dialogue. A second set of quotation marks is used after the last word of dialogue.

      "I love to sail."               "Is the fruit ripe**?**"

If the dialogue does not end the sentence, put a comma (not a period) inside the quotation marks. The period belongs at the very end of the sentence.

      "I love to sail," Chloe said.      "The fruit isn't ripe," said Geoff.

If the dialogue is a question and does not end the sentence, keep the question mark inside the quotation marks.

      "Do you love sailing**?**" Chloe asked.

      "Are the bananas ripe**?**" asked Geoff.

If part of the sentence comes before the dialogue, put a comma after that part of the sentence. The period at the end of the sentence belongs inside the quotation marks.

      Chloe said, "I love to sail."      Geoff asked, "Is the fruit ripe**?**"

## Proof It

Read each sentence below. If the sentence is correct, make a check mark on the line (✓). If it is not correct, make an **X** on the line. Then, use the proofreading marks in the box to show the changes.

| | |
|---|---|
| ∧ | = insert comma |
| ⊙ | = insert period |
| ᐯ | = insert quotation marks |

Example: __**X**__ ᐯOur suitcases are in the attic∧" said Dad⊙

1. _____ This summer, I am going to take Spanish lessons, said Mackenzie.

2. _____ "My family is driving all the way across the country in an RV," Ryan said.

3. _____ Nicolae said "I plan to go swimming at the lake every day

# Lesson 2.12 Punctuating Dialogue

## Rewrite It

The sentences below are missing commas, periods, and quotation marks.
Rewrite each sentence. Add punctuation marks where needed.

1. I have never been to a farm before replied Audrey

    _____

2. Neither have I agreed Nicolae

    _____

3. My grandparents have cows, horses, goats, and barn cats said Van

    _____

4. He added I stay with them every summer, and there is always
   something to do

    _____

5. I would love to learn how to ride a horse or milk a cow said Audrey

    _____

6. Van grinned at Audrey and said My grandparents can always use an
   extra hand

    _____

## Try It

Ask two of your classmates what they plan to do next summer. Record their
answers on the lines below. Remember to use quotation marks to show the
exact words your classmates use.

1. _____

2. _____

# Lesson 2.13 Punctuating Titles

**Titles of books, movies, and plays** are underlined.

Lucas did a book report on <u>Two Heads Are Better Than One</u>.

The movie <u>Two Brothers</u> is an adventure about twin tiger cubs.

For Dionne's birthday, her family went to see the play <u>Peter Pan</u>.

**Titles of songs, poems, and stories** are set in quotation marks.

Judith Viorst wrote the poem "If I Were in Charge of the World."

The story "The Emperor's Clothes" is in my book of fairy tales.

My favorite song is "Bright Eyes" by Remy Zero.

## Complete It

Read each sentence below. Underline the titles of books, movies, and plays. Put quotation marks around the titles of songs, stories, and poems.

1. Before the first softball game of the season, we always sing Take Me Out to the Ballgame.

2. Scotty Smalls is the main character in the movie The Sandlot.

3. My favorite poem is Eletelephony by Laura E. Richards.

4. In the play Annie, Bridget McCabe had the lead role.

5. Laura Ingalls Wilder wrote Little House in the Big Woods.

6. The movie The Incredibles won an award for Best Animated Film.

7. When it was time for bed, Dad told me a story called Gregory and Grandpa's Wild Balloon Ride.

8. I memorized Edward Lear's poem The Owl and the Pussycat.

9. Singing the song Purple People Eater makes my sister laugh.

| Tip | Remember to place periods inside quotation marks if a title comes at the end of a sentence. |
|---|---|

## Lesson 2.13 Punctuating Titles

**Proof It**

Read the diary entry below. Find the titles, and underline them or place them in quotation marks. To add quotation marks, use this symbol (v).

                                              Thursday, October 8

Dear Diary,

         I had a very busy week. On Monday, I went to the library after school. I worked on the story I am writing. It is called The Mystery of the Golden Toothbrush. I borrowed the books Summer of the Sea Serpent, Stone Fox, and Pink and Say. I am going to write a book report on one of them, but I haven't decided which one.

         On Wednesday, I recited two poems for Poetry Week. I chose The Shadow by Robert Louis Stevenson and Jellyfish Stew by Jack Prelutsky. After school, I tried out for the play The Princess and the Pea. I hope I land the role of the princess.

         On Friday night, Ankit and Kendra came over to watch some movies. We rented Antz and My Neighbor Totoro. Antz is Kendra's favorite movie. My parents made subs and popcorn for us. We had a lot of fun, but I'm glad this crazy week is over!

**Try It**

1. What is your favorite song? Write the title on the line.

_____

2. Think of an idea for a story you could write. Then, write two possible titles for your story on the lines below.

_____

_____

## Review Punctuating Dialogue and Titles

The exact words a person says are called **dialogue**. Quotation marks are used with dialogue.

"My piano recital is on Saturday."     "Where are my shoes?"

If the dialogue does not end the sentence, put a comma inside the quotation marks (unless it is a question mark). Put a period at the end of the sentence.

"My piano recital is on Saturday," said Bella.

"Where are my shoes?" John asked.

If part of the sentence comes before the dialogue, put a comma after it. Put the end mark at the end of the sentence inside the quotation marks.

Bella said, "My piano recital is on Saturday."

John asked, "Where are my shoes?"

Titles of books, movies, and plays are underlined. Titles of songs, poems, and stories are set in quotation marks.

Camden Little Theater is producing the play <u>The Selfish Giant</u>.

Meera named her story "A Day in the Life of a Hamster."

### Putting It Together

Read the sentences below. Use proofreading marks to add commas, periods, and quotation marks where they are needed.

| | |
|---|---|
| ∧ | = insert comma |
| ⊙ | = insert period |
| ˅ | = insert quotation marks |

1. I have a pen pal who lives in France, said Louie.

2. I know a few words in French, and he knows a little English he added

3. Sarah Kate said "My pen pal is from Australia.

4. "Language probably is not a problem, then" replied Louie

5. Sarah Kate laughed and said "No, it isn't, but I do get to learn some great Aussie expressions"

# Review  Punctuating Dialogue and Titles

Read the schedule below. Decide whether titles should be underlined or set in quotation marks. Then, mark them correctly.

---

### Schedule of Events for the Beaver River Kids' Center

| | |
|---|---|
| August 4–10 | See the touching story of Sadako in the play A Thousand Cranes. |
| August 18 | Come to a special double-feature of the movies A Little Princess and Because of Winn-Dixie. |
| August 24 | Listen to Ian Nelson perform favorite poems like Us Two by A. A. Milne, Someone's Toes Are in My Nose by Bruce Lansky, and Catch a Little Rhyme by Eve Merriam. |
| September 4 | Meet famous author Ramona Darling. She'll be signing copies of her new book, At the Top of the Cherry Tree. |
| September 12 | Audition for the play The Legend of Sleepy Hollow. |
| September 23 | Come and listen to the band Foot-Stomping Blues perform favorite songs, like No Time for Crying and Going to the Moon. |

---

Read each pair of sentences below. Choose the correct version of each sentence. Write its letter on the line.

1. _____ **a.** Eli's book <u>Jake Drake, Bully Buster</u> is overdue at the library.
   **b.** Eli's book "Jake Drake, Bully Buster" is overdue at the library.

2. _____ **a.** "Mom and I are going to the pool said Alicia."
   **b.** "Mom and I are going to the pool," said Alicia.

3. _____ **a.** Aunt Daisy said. "Don't forget to bring the cupcakes with you,"
   **b.** Aunt Daisy said, "Don't forget to bring the cupcakes with you."

4. _____ **a.** The story "The Adventures of Robin & Delilah" won first prize.
   **b.** The story <u>The Adventures of Robin & Delilah</u> won first prize.

The **subject** of a sentence tells who or what the sentence is about. When the subject is **singular**, it is only one person, place, or thing. When there is a singular subject, the verb ends with **s** or **es**.

Add **s** to most regular verbs that have a single subject.

*The boat* sail**s** close to shore.     *The woman* water**s** the flower.

Add **es** to regular verbs that have a single subject and end in **sh**, **ch**, **s**, **x**, and **z**.

*Gran* kiss**es** us good-bye.     *Jake* crunch**es** his cereal loudly.

When the subject is **plural**, it is more than one person, place, or thing. When the subject is plural, the verb does not end with **s** or **es**.

*The kittens* sleep on the sofa.     *Zared and Nina* latch the gate.

**Proof It**

Read the paragraph below. Underline the subjects. Find the verbs that do not agree with their subjects. Add or delete **s** or **es** from the verbs so that they agree with their subjects. Use this symbol (^) to add a letter or letters. Cross out letters that don't belong.

Mr. Ruskin wash his historic car on Saturdays. Aaron and Ali helps him. Mr. Ruskin sprays the old car with warm water. He scrub every inch of the car with a big sponge. The children polishes the windshield and the mirrors. They use clean, soft rags. Aaron wax the beautiful red car. It shine in the sunlight. He wishes to have a car just like his dad's one day. Mr. Ruskin take Aaron and Ali for a drive in the shiny car every Saturday afternoon. They buy ice-cream cones. Then, they walks in the park.

# Lesson 3.1 Subject-Verb Agreement: Adding **s** and **es**

## Complete It

Read each sentence below. Then, read the pair of verbs in parentheses ( ). Choose the correct verb form. Write it on the line.

1. Emily and Mateo _____ a ball in the backyard. (toss, tosses)

2. The Jorgenson's _____ their pumpkins every autumn. (harvest, harvests)

3. My little brother _____ his teeth with an electric toothbrush. (brush, brushes)

4. Britta _____ ten miles a day when she is in training for the race. (bike, bikes)

5. The blender _____ the ingredients. (mix, mixes)

6. The Guzmans _____ near a crystal-clear mountain lake every summer. (camp, camps)

7. The shaggy Irish setter _____ the ball each time I throw it. (catch, catches)

8. Aunt Celeste _____ about two hours away. (live, lives)

## Try It

1. Write a sentence using one of the following verbs: *climb, skate, twirl, travel, race, point,* or *bake.* Underline the subject in your sentence, and circle the verb. Make sure that the subject and the verb agree.

_____

2. Write a sentence using one of the following verbs *push, crash, finish, pitch, watch, miss,* or *fix.* Underline the subject in your sentence, and circle the verb. Make sure that the subject and the verb agree.

_____

## Lesson 3.2 Irregular Verbs: *Am, Is, Are*

*Am, is,* and *are* are all different forms of the verb *to be*.

*Am* is used only with the subject *I*.

    *I **am** sleepy.   I **am** hungry.   I **am** under the bed.*

*Is* is used when the subject is singular.

    *Mickey **is** sixteen.   Annabelle **is** tall.   The beach **is** rocky.*

*Are* is used with the subject *you*.

    *You **are** very funny.   You **are** correct.   You **are** first in line.*

*Are* is also used when the subject is plural.

    *Haley Joel Osment and Dakota Fanning **are** actors.*
    *The boys **are** at home.*

### Rewrite It

Rewrite each sentence below. If it has a plural subject, rewrite it with
a single subject. If it has a single subject, rewrite it with a plural subject.
Remember that the form of the verb must agree with the subject and verb.

Example: The salad dressing and the salad are on the table.

    The salad dressing is on the table.

1. Nissa and Toby are eight.

   _____

2. The photograph is in an album.

   _____

3. The CDs on the shelf are from the library.

   _____

4. We are excited about traveling to Mexico.

   _____

## Lesson 3.2 Irregular Verbs: *Am, Is, Are*

**Proof It**

Read the paragraphs below. There are 11 mistakes with the verbs *am, is,* and *are*. Cross out each mistake. Then, write the correct form of the verb above it.

A topiary (*toe pee air ee*) are a kind of sculpture made from plants. Topiaries is cut to look like many different things. Some am shaped like animals. For example, a topiary can look like an elephant, a bear, a horse, or even a dinosaur. Other topiaries is trimmed to look like castles, cones, or mazes.

A topiary gardener are an artist. He or she can turn simple shrubs into beautiful sculptures. Boxwood, holly, bay laurel, and yew am some of the best plants to use for topiary. They is easy to train and to trim.

In May, I are going to visit the Green Animals Topiary Garden in Rhode Island. It am one of the oldest topiary gardens in the country. There am 80 pieces of topiary there! It are fun to imagine all the green animals coming to life and roaming the gardens.

**Try It**

Write three sentences on the lines below. Use the verbs *am, is,* or *are* in each sentence.

_____

_____

_____

## Lesson 3.3  Irregular Verbs: *Has, Have*

*Has* and *have* are different forms of the verb *to have*.

*Have* is used when the subject is *I* or *you*.

    *I **have** a cold.*               *You **have** two brothers.*

*Have* is also used with plural subjects.

    *We **have** a book about dinosaurs.*

    *Roberto and Chiara **have** a baby sister.*

    *They **have** a yellow house.*       *Both cars **have** flat tires.*

*Has* is used when there is a single subject like *he, she,* or *it*.

    *She **has** blonde hair.*         *The librarian **has** a cheerful smile.*

    *A male deer **has** antlers.*

### Complete It

Complete each sentence below with the word *has* or *have*. Write the correct word in the space.

1. Gus and Emily _____ a shell collection.

2. A horse conch _____ a cone shape and can grow to be almost two feet long.

3. Shells _____ value when they are beautiful or rare.

4. The shapes of some shells _____ interesting names, like helmet, basket, lamp, frog, and trumpet.

5. Oysters and clams _____ shells that are hinged at the back.

6. Emily _____ a necklace made from polished pieces of shell.

7. Cowrie shells _____ been used as money on Indian and Pacific islands.

8. If Gus _____ more than one of a certain shell, he will trade it with other collectors.

## Lesson 3.3 Irregular Verbs: *Has, Have*

**Proof It**

Read the letter below. There are eight mistakes with the verbs *have* and *has*. Cross out each incorrect verb. Then, write the correct form of the verb above it.

---

August 6, 2015

Dear Kyra,

How is life at home in Massachusetts? We are having a great time in Florida. Gus and I has 40 new shells to add to our collection! We has been busy searching the beaches here. Gus and I already has labels for our new shells. We don't want to forget their names by the time we get home.

Some shells still has animals living in them. We never collect those shells. Our parents has helped us look in rock crevices and tide pools. That is how we found a true tulip shell. It have a pretty peachy color and an interesting pattern.

I has a surprise to bring home for you. You has never seen a shell like this. I can't wait to see you. Wish you were here!

Your friend,

Emily

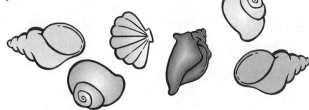

---

# Review | Subject-Verb Agreement and Irregular Verbs

Add **s** to most regular verbs that have a **single subject**. Add **es** to regular verbs that have a single subject and end in **sh, ch, s, x,** or **z.**

> *The plane* take**s** off from the first runway.
> *Anthony* pitch**es** the ball.

When the subject is **plural**, the verb does not end with **s** or **es**.

> *The daffodils* bloom in April.

*Am, is,* and *are* are forms of the verb *to be.*
Use *am* with the subject *I.*

> *I **am** glad.*
> *I **am** on my way to school.*

Use *is* when the subject is singular.

> *Ms. Caldero **is** a musician.*

Use *are* with the subject *you.* Also use *are* when the subject is plural.

> *You **are** the only one who understands.*
> *The coins **are** in my piggybank.*

*Has* and *have* are different forms of the verb *to have.*

*Have* is used when the subject is *I* or *you.*

> *I **have** a guinea pig named Moe.*
> *You **have** the chicken pox.*

*Have* is also used with plural subjects.

> *William and Dante **have** blue bicycles.*
> *Huskies **have** thick fur and curly tails.*

*Has* is used when there is a single subject.

> *The train **has** a red caboose.*
> *Nadia **has** eight cousins.*

# Review — Subject-Verb Agreement and Irregular Verbs

## Putting It Together

Read the paragraphs below. Cross out each incorrect verb. Then, write the correct form of the verb above it. You will find eight mistakes.

The Everglades cover about 4,000 square miles of land. They is located in southwestern Florida. Marshes and swamps makes up a large part of the Everglades. They are covered with saw grass. It grow to be about 15 feet tall. People cannot easily reaches much of the Everglades because the saw grass am so thick. This area are sometimes called *the river of grass*.

The Everglades have many different kinds of plants and wildlife. The tropical area makes a good home for birds like herons, egrets, spoonbills, and pelicans. The Everglades are the only place in the world that has both crocodiles and alligators. Deer, panthers, otters, and manatees makes their homes there, too. Quiet visitors catches a glimpse of many animals.

Read each sentence below. Then, circle the verb from the pair in parentheses ( ) that best completes each sentence.

1. The black snake (hiss, hisses) at the nearby raptor.

2. Palms, pines, and cypresses (grow, grows) in the Everglades.

3. An alligator (has, have) a wide, flat snout, and a crocodile (has, have) a narrow snout.

4. The park ranger (watch, watches) people to make sure they stay safe.

5. Dragonflies (gather, gathers) their food while they fly.

## Lesson 3.4   Forming the Past Tense by Adding **ed**

Verbs in the **present tense** tell about things that are happening right now. Verbs in the **past tense** tell about things that have already happened.

Add **ed** to a regular verb to change it to the past tense. If the verb already ends in **e**, just add **d**.

> The concert end**ed** at 9:00.     It snow**ed** 16 inches yesterday!
> Uncle Donny taste**d** the pudding.  The waitress smile**d** at the girl.

If a verb ends in **y**, change the **y** to **i** and add **ed**.

> We hur**ry** to catch the bus.     We hur**ried** to catch the bus.
> I d**ry** the laundry outside.      I d**ried** the laundry outside.

**Complete It**

Read the sentences below. Complete each sentence with the past tense of the verb in parentheses ( ).

1. Leonardo da Vinci _____ the mysterious *Mona Lisa*. (paint)

2. Women and children often _____ for artist Mary Cassatt. (pose)

3. The Impressionists _____ the world that not all paintings had to look realistic. (show)

4. Grandma Moses _____ to paint cheerful pictures of life in the country. (love)

5. Jackson Pollack, who made colorful paint-splattered paintings, _____ with Thomas Hart Benton. (study)

6. Vincent van Gogh _____ more than 800 oil paintings during his lifetime! (create)

7. Chinese artist Wang Yani _____ painting when she was only two. (start)

## Lesson 3.4   Forming the Past Tense by Adding **ed**

**Rewrite It**

Read the sentences below. They are all in the present tense. Underline the verb in each sentence. Then, rewrite the sentences in the past tense.

1. Norman Rockwell lives from 1894 until 1978.

   _____

2. Norman studies at the National Academy of Design in New York.

   _____

3. He illustrates issues of children's magazines, like *Boys' Life*.

   _____

4. Norman paints scenes from everyday small town life.

   _____

5. Norman calls himself a storyteller.

   _____

6. A fire destroys many of Norman's paintings.

   _____

7. Norman Rockwell receives the Presidential Medal of Freedom in 1976.

   _____

**Try It**

1. Write a sentence in the present tense that describes a piece of art you have seen or made.

   _____

2. Now, rewrite the same sentence in the past tense.

   _____

## Lesson 3.5  Irregular Past-Tense Verbs: *Ate, Said, Grew, Made, Rode*

Some verbs do not follow the pattern of regular verbs. The past tenses of these verbs are different. To form the past tense, do not add **ed** or **d** to these verbs. Instead, you must change the entire word.

| **Present Tense** | **Past Tense** |
|---|---|
| She *eats* a snack every day. | She *ate* a snack every day. |
| Mario *says* it will rain tonight. | Mario *said* it will rain tonight. |
| The tiny pine tree *grows* quickly. | The tiny pine tree *grew* quickly. |
| Catalina *makes* bracelets. | Catalina *made* bracelets. |
| I *ride* the bus downtown. | I *rode* the bus downtown. |

**Proof It**

Some of the verbs below are in the wrong tense. Cross out the verbs in bold type. Use this symbol (^), and write the correct word above it.

When my mom was a little girl, her family owned a bakery. Mom **says** that she loved the sweet smell of bread and pastries baking in the ovens. Every morning, Mom **eats** a cinnamon roll for breakfast. She **rides** her bike to school when the weather was nice. In her bag, she carried fresh muffins for her teachers and her friends.

In the afternoon, she and her dad **make** crusty rolls and chewy bagels. Grandpa put all the ingredients in a big bowl. He and Mom took turns kneading the dough. Then, he covered it with a clean towel. The dough **grows** and **grows**. Mom **says** she loved to punch it down. Finally, she and Grandpa shaped the dough and popped it into the ovens. Mom's family **eats** fresh bread with dinner every night!

## Lesson 3.5 Irregular Past-Tense Verbs: *Ate, Said, Grew, Made, Rode*

**Solve It**

Read each sentence below. On the line, write the past tense of the underlined verb.

1. Grandma always <u>eats</u> a blueberry bagel with cream cheese for breakfast. _____

2. The Larsons <u>say</u> that Hot Cross Buns was the best bakery in town.

   _____

3. Mom's cousin, Eddie, <u>rides</u> his bike around town and delivered bread.

   _____

4. Mom <u>grows</u> up helping her parents at the bakery. _____

5. Every Saturday, Mom and Grandpa <u>make</u> 12 loaves of wheat bread, 15 loaves of French bread, and 100 dinner rolls. _____

| h | q | s | a | i | d | r |
|---|---|---|---|---|---|---|
| m | p | n | t | m | a | l |
| z | g | r | e | w | g | k |
| u | d | k | y | f | l | g |
| j | h | v | r | u | a | e |
| i | b | b | o | w | d | y |
| t | m | a | d | e | x | c |
| j | s | f | e | p | p | e |

Now, find each past-tense verb in the word search puzzle. Circle the words you find. Words are written across and down.

**Try It**

1. What did you eat for dinner last night? Use a complete sentence to answer the question.

   _____

2. Write a sentence that uses the past tense of one of these words: *say, grow, make,* or *ride*.

   _____

## Lesson 3.6 Irregular Past-Tense Verbs: *Gave, Flew, Brought, Thought, Wrote*

The past tenses of some verbs do not follow the patterns of regular verbs. To form the past tense, do not add **ed** or **d**. Instead, you must change the entire word.

**Present Tense**
Franklin *gives* her an orange.
The goose *flies* over the pond.
Marisa *brings* some games.
Beth *thinks* she got an A.
I *write* a letter to my grandma.

**Past Tense**
Franklin *gave* her an orange.
The goose *flew* over the pond.
Marisa *brought* some games.
Beth *thought* she got an A.
I *wrote* a letter to my grandma.

**Rewrite It**
The sentences below are all in the present tense. Rewrite them in the past tense.

1. Ms. Lucetta gives the class an assignment.

_____

2. Nicholas and Liv write a play about a giant who lives in the forest.

_____

3. They think the giant should be kind, not scary.

_____

4. A small bluebird flies many miles to save the kind giant.

_____

5. The bluebird brings him an important message.

_____

6. The giant gives the bluebird shelter in his cave.

_____

## Lesson 3.6  Irregular Past-Tense Verbs: *Gave, Flew, Brought, Thought, Wrote*

### Proof It

Some of the verbs below are in the wrong tense. Cross out the underlined verbs. Use this symbol (^), and write the correct past-tense verbs above them.

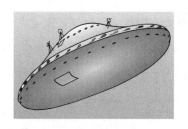

Pradeep and Kent <u>write</u> a play for Ms. Lucetta's class. Their play was about a brother and sister who <u>think</u> that an alien spaceship landed near their house. They named the brother and sister Harry and Carrie. In the play, something very large <u>flies</u> over Harry and Carrie's house one night. It made a loud whirring noise. Its lights flashed on and off.

Carrie ran to the window. She <u>thinks</u> it was a helicopter until she saw how big it was. Harry ran into the backyard. He <u>brings</u> his camera with him. Harry took as many photos as he could. Then, the ship grew silent and quickly <u>flies</u> away.

Pradeep and Kent <u>think</u> the play they <u>write</u> was fun and exciting. They were not sure how to end it though. Did aliens actually visit Harry and Carrie's house? Was it all a dream? They knew they would have to decide before they <u>give</u> their play to Ms. Lucetta.

### Try It

In the selection above, why did the spaceship fly away? Use the past tense of the verb *fly* in your answer.

_____

## Lesson 3.7　Forming the Future Tense

To write or speak about something that is happening right now, use the **present tense**. When something has already happened, use the **past tense**. When something has not happened yet, use the **future tense**.

> **Past:** I *used* all the shampoo.
> **Present:** I *use* all the shampoo.
> **Future:** I *will use* all the shampoo.

The future tense is formed by using the word *will* with a verb. The word *will* means that something has not taken place yet, but it will happen in the future.

> Seamus *will come* home in three days.
> The plumber *will fix* the leaky pipe.
> The water *will boil* in a minute or two.
> Ms. Webster *will make* lasagna for dinner.

### Complete It

Complete each sentence with the future tense of the verb in parentheses ( ).

1. Charlotte _____ a doctor when she grows up. (be)

2. Fernando _____ to speak eight languages. (learn)

3. Maddy _____ for the Olympics. (train)

4. Travis _____ a cure for a serious disease. (find)

5. Akio _____ wild animals. (photograph)

6. Elena _____ all around the world. (travel)

## Lesson 3.7  Forming the Future Tense

**Rewrite It**

On the line, write **PA** if a sentence takes place in the past. Write **PR** if it takes place in the present. Then, rewrite each sentence in the future tense.

Example: _PA_ The movie ended at 8:00.

_The movie will end at 8:00._

1. _____ The sheepdog barked at the mail carrier.

_____

2. _____ The gardener picks flowers from her wildflower garden.

_____

3. _____ The robin pulls a fat earthworm from the soil.

_____

4. _____ A ladybug landed on Layla's shoulder.

_____

**Try It**

1. Write a sentence about someplace you have been in the past. Underline the verb.

_____

2. Write a sentence about where you are right now. Underline the verb.

_____

3. Write a sentence about somewhere you will go or something you will do in the future. Underline the verb.

_____

# Review | Regular and Irregular Past-Tense Verbs and Future-Tense Verbs

Change a regular verb to the **past tense** by adding **ed**. If the verb already ends in **e**, just add **d**.

elect → elect**ed**          explore → explore**d**          taste → taste**d**

If a verb ends in **y**, change the **y** to **i** and add **ed**.

study → stud**ied**          worry → worr**ied**          carry → carr**ied**

For verbs that do not follow this pattern, do not add **ed** or **d**. Instead, change the entire word.

give → gave          bring → brought          fly → flew
think → thought      write → wrote            eat → ate
say → said           grow → grew              make → made
ride → rode

The **future tense** is formed by using the word *will* with a verb. Use the future tense to write or speak about things that have not happened yet.

Janie *will set* the table.          Armando *will help*.

## Putting It Together

Rewrite each sentence below in a different tense. The word in parentheses ( ) tells you which tense to use.

1. Wilbur and Orville Wright dream of flying. (past)

_____

2. The Wright Brothers will fly the first manned plane in 1903. (past)

_____

3. My family and I visited Kitty Hawk—the site of the first flight. (future)

_____

4. I wrote about our trips in my journal. (present)

_____

# Review — Regular and Irregular Past-Tense Verbs and Future-Tense Verbs

Read each sentence below. In the space, write the past tense of the underlined verb.

1. Wilbur and Orville Wright <u>study</u> how birds flew. _____

2. They <u>test</u> many different kinds of wings. _____

3. The brothers <u>try</u> to use gliders, but the gliders weren't strong enough to carry a person. _____

4. The *Wright Flyer* <u>uses</u> a propeller to move. _____

5. Many people <u>think</u> that humans would never fly. _____

6. For 20 years, London's Science Museum <u>displays</u> the first plane.

   _____

7. They <u>give</u> the plane to the Smithsonian's National Museum of Space in 1948. _____

Cross out the verb in each sentence below. Then, use this symbol (^) and write the future tense above it.

1. The flight attendant offered us juice and pretzels.

2. The pilot greets all the passengers.

3. I look out the tiny window at the towns and rivers far below.

4. The world seems peaceful from thousands of feet above the ground.

5. The girl beside me listened to her CD player for most of the flight.

6. The airplane landed at 7:00.

7. It arrives an hour late.

## Lesson 3.8  Contractions with *Not, Will,* and *Have*

A **contraction** is a short way of saying something by combining two words into one. An apostrophe (') takes the place of the missing letters.

Many contractions are formed when a verb and the word *not* are combined. The apostrophe takes the place of the letter **o** in *not*.

| | | |
|---|---|---|
| is not = isn't | are not = aren't | was not = wasn't |
| were not = weren't | does not = doesn't | did not = didn't |
| do not = don't | can not = can't | |

Some contractions can be formed with pronouns and the verb *will*. An apostrophe takes the place of the letters **wi** in *will*.

| | | |
|---|---|---|
| I will = I'll | it will = it'll | you will = you'll |
| we will = we'll | she will = she'll | they will = they'll |
| he will = he'll | | |

Contractions can also be made with the verb *have*. An apostrophe takes the place of the letters **ha** in *have*.

| | |
|---|---|
| I have = I've | we have = we've |
| you have = you've | they have = they've |

**Proof It**

Cross out the five incorrect contractions below. Use this proofreading mark (^), and write the correct contraction above it.

My neighborhood is having a giant yard sale on Saturday. Wel'l post signs all around town. This week, I'ill go through the boxes under my bed and in the attic. There are many things I know we do'nt need. At first, my little brother did'nt want to help. Then, I told him all the money would go to the animal shelter where we got our dog Maisy. I think he'ill be happy to help now.

## Lesson 3.8 Contractions with *Not, Will,* and *Have*

### Rewrite It

Circle the two words in each sentence that could be combined to make a contraction. Then, rewrite the sentences using contractions.

1. We were not even open for business yet when the first customers arrived.

_____

2. "I will give you 15 dollars for the tricycle," said Mrs. Smythe.

_____

3. "You will find many great bargains," Justin told our customers.

_____

4. Our free lemonade did not last long.

_____

5. We have raised hundreds of dollars for the animal shelter!

_____

6. Maisy and I can not wait to give the check to the shelter's director.

_____

### Try It

1. Write a sentence about something you do not like doing. Use a contraction with *not* in your sentence. Circle the contraction.

_____

2. Write a sentence about something you will do in the future. Use a contraction with *will* in your sentence. Circle the contraction.

_____

## Lesson 3.9  Contractions with *Am*, *Is*, *Are*, and *Would*

**Contractions** can be made with different forms of the verb *to be*. The apostrophe takes the place of the first vowel in *am*, *is*, and *are*.

| | |
|---|---|
| I am = I'm | it is = it's |
| you are = you're | we are = we're |
| he is = he's | they are = they're |
| she is = she's | |

Contractions formed with the word *would* are a little different. The apostrophe takes the place of the entire word, except for the **d**.

| | |
|---|---|
| I would = I'd | it would = it'd |
| you would = you'd | we would = we'd |
| he would = he'd | they would = they'd |
| she would = she'd | |

**Match It**

Match each pair of underlined words with its contraction. Write the letter of the contraction in the space.

1. _____ <u>I am</u> going to take gymnastics lessons with my friend, Elise.

2. _____ <u>She is</u> a year older than I am.

3. _____ Elise said <u>she would</u> show me some warm-up stretches.

4. _____ Our class meets on Wednesdays. <u>It is</u> in an old building on Fourth Street.

5. _____ <u>We are</u> going to carpool to class.

6. _____ Elise's dad teaches gymnastics. <u>He is</u> also the high school coach.

7. _____ <u>I would</u> like to be on his team when I am in high school.

**a.** We're

**b.** she'd

**c.** He's

**d.** I'm

**e.** I'd

**f.** It's

**g.** She's

## Lesson 3.9   Contractions with *Am, Is, Are,* and *Would*

**Complete It**

Fill in each blank below with a contraction from the box.

| I'm | It's | He's | It'd |
|---|---|---|---|
| We're | she'd | I'd | She's |

1. _____ like to meet Olympic gold-medal gymnast Carly Patterson one day.

2. _____ from my hometown of Baton Rouge, Louisiana.

3. In an interview, Carly said _____ like to try a career in singing.

4. Elise's favorite gymnast is Blaine Wilson. _____ a three-time Olympic gymnast.

5. _____ each going to write a letter to Carly and Blaine.

6. _____ sure they will write back to us when they hear what big fans we are.

7. _____ be an amazing experience to see the Olympic Games live.

8. _____ my dream to travel to the 2016 Olympics.

**Try It**

1. Write a sentence about a famous person you would like to meet. Use a contraction in your sentence. Underline the contraction.

_____

2. Write a sentence that includes a contraction with the word *am, is,* or *are.* Underline the contraction.

_____

# Lesson 3.10 Negative Words and Double Negatives

**Negative words** are words like *no, none, never, nothing, nobody, nowhere,* and *no one.* The word *not* and contractions that use *not* are also negative words. A sentence needs only one negative word. It is incorrect to use a **double negative,** or more than one negative word, in a sentence.

> **Correct:** There were *not* any oranges in the refrigerator.
> There were *no* oranges in the refrigerator.
> **Incorrect:** There were *not no* oranges in the refrigerator.

> **Correct:** Kevin *never* saw anyone he knew at the store.
> Kevin saw *no one* he knew at the store.
> **Incorrect:** Kevin *never* saw *no one* he knew at the store.

> **Correct:** *None* of the students were born in another country.
> **Incorrect:** *None* of the students *weren't* born in another country.

## Proof It

Read the paragraphs below. There are five double negatives. Cross out one negative word or phrase in the incorrect sentences to correct them.

If you haven't never heard of Jellyfish Lake, you should learn more about it. This amazing saltwater lake is in Palau, an island in the Philippines. You do not never want to get too close to a jellyfish in the ocean. Ocean jellyfish sting their prey. The jellyfish of Jellyfish Lake do not have no stingers. Instead, they use algae and sunlight to get the nutrients they need.

These jellyfish have only one predator—the sea anemone. This is why there are so many of them. No one can never swim in the lake without seeing millions of these jellyfish. It is a special experience for humans. Not nowhere else in the world can people swim surrounded by more than 25 million harmless jellyfish.

## Lesson 3.10 Negative Words and Double Negatives

**Complete It**

Read each sentence below. Circle the word or words from the pair in parentheses ( ) that correctly complete each sentence.

1. The jellyfish don't (never, ever) stop moving.

2. They don't do (anything, nothing) but follow the sun across the lake all day long.

3. My aunt said there (is, is not) nowhere on Earth she would rather go snorkeling.

4. People who swim with the jellyfish shouldn't (ever, never) lift or throw the delicate animals.

5. There aren't (no, any) jellyfish without stingers in the oceans of the world.

6. Because the jellyfish don't have to hunt for their food, there (was, was not) no need for stingers.

7. The beautiful jellyfish don't (never, ever) seem to be too bothered by human visitors.

8. El Niño brought high temperatures to Palau in the late 1990s. Suddenly, there weren't (any, no) jellyfish in the lake.

**Try It**

1. Write a sentence using one of these negative words: *no, none, never, nothing, nobody, nowhere, no one,* or *not.*

_____

2. On another piece of paper, write a sentence using a double negative. Trade papers with a classmate. On the line below, write your classmate's sentence correctly.

# Review | Contractions, Negative Words, and Double Negatives

A **contraction** is a short way of saying something by combining two words into one. An apostrophe (') takes the place of the missing letters.

Some contractions are formed with a verb and the word *not*.

         is not = isn't         were not = weren't         do not = don't

Other contractions are combinations of pronouns with the verbs *will*, *have*, *am*, *is*, *are*, and *would*.

         we will = we'll         you have = you've         I am = I'm
         it is = it's         we are = we're         you would = you'd

Do not use more than one negative word, *no, not, none, never, nothing, nobody, nowhere*, and *no one*, in a sentence. This includes contractions with *not*.

> **Correct:** The Cougars *haven't* lost any games this season.
> **Incorrect:** The Cougars *haven't* lost *no* games this season.

## Putting It Together

Read the paragraph below. Cross out the five incorrect contractions. Use this symbol (^), and write the correct contractions above them. Then, find the two double negatives, and correct them.

Ghost towns arent the strong, lively towns they used to be. The'yve changed because people and businesses have moved away. Most ghost towns are in the West. Many of them used to be mining towns. When there was'nt anything left to mine, the towns dried up. Towns that havent' changed since the 1800s can be fun to explore. But dont expect to take home no souvenirs. No one is allowed to take nothing from the towns— except for photographs.

**Review** # Contractions, Negative Words, and Double Negatives

Match each pair of underlined words with its contraction. Write the letter of the contraction on the line.

1. _____ Do not explore a ghost town without a map and plenty of water.

2. _____ The guide said it is not a good idea to get too close to mine openings.

3. _____ She is an expert in ghost towns of the West.

4. _____ We did not want to miss seeing Tombstone, Jerome, and Wolf Hole.

5. _____ They are located in Arizona—so are more than 250 other ghost towns!

6. _____ I have put together an album of the ghost towns I have visited.

7. _____ I think you would enjoy learning the histories of these deserted towns.

a. I've

b. isn't

c. didn't

d. you'd

e. Don't

f. They're

g. She's

Read each pair of sentences. Make a check mark (✓) next to each sentence that uses negative words correctly.

1. _____ Some towns don't never recover when a mine closes.
   _____ Some towns don't ever recover when a mine closes.

2. _____ There are not any buildings left in some abandoned towns.
   _____ There are not no buildings left in some abandoned towns.

3. _____ Dad says there isn't nowhere like ghost towns for learning about life in the Old West.
   _____ Dad says there is nowhere like ghost towns for learning about life in the Old West.

## Lesson 3.11 Forming Plurals with **s** and **es**

The word **plural** means *more than one*. To make many nouns plural, add **s**.

one egg → two egg**s**           one dog → six dog**s**

one pencil → many pencil**s**       one photo → nine photo**s**

If a noun ends in **sh**, **ch**, **s**, or **x**, form the plural by adding **es**.

one bu**sh** → three bush**es**        one pea**ch** → five peach**es**

one fo**x** → two fox**es**          one bu**s** → several bus**es**

If a noun ends with a consonant and a **y**, drop the **y** and add **ies** to form the plural.

one bab**y** → all the bab**ies**        one cit**y** → many cit**ies**

### Complete It

Read each sentence below. Complete it with the plural form of the word in parentheses ( ).

1. Ethan made two _____ as he blew out his birthday candles. (wish)

2. All the _____ in the yard came down during the huge thunderstorm last week. (branch)

3. Jacob takes care of the _____ next door when our neighbors go out of town. (cat)

4. We need about six ripe _____ to make apple pie. (apple)

5. Hallie left her _____ at a friend's house. (glass)

6. Claudia and Crista picked sour _____ from the tree in the yard. (cherry)

7. Please recycle the _____ in the garage. (box)

8. Four _____ have volunteered to organize the book sale. (family)

## Lesson 3.11 Forming Plurals with **s** and **es**

**Solve It**

Read the clues below. Find the word in the box that matches each clue. Then, make the word plural, and write it in the numbered space in the crossword puzzle.

airplane     dress
bed     beach
giraffe     fox
dish     baby

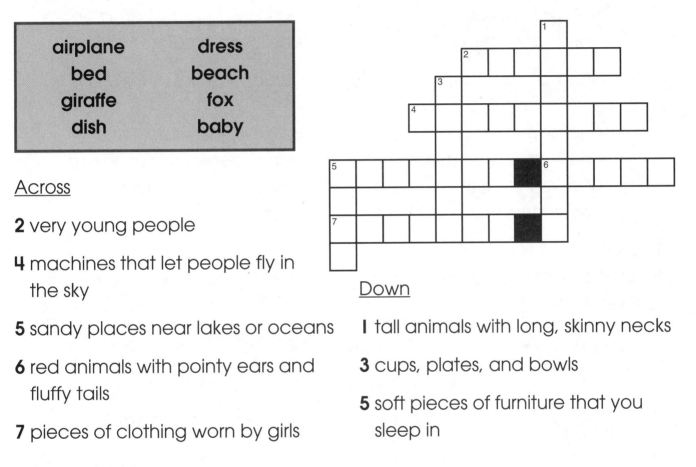

Across

**2** very young people

**4** machines that let people fly in the sky

**5** sandy places near lakes or oceans

**6** red animals with pointy ears and fluffy tails

**7** pieces of clothing worn by girls

Down

**1** tall animals with long, skinny necks

**3** cups, plates, and bowls

**5** soft pieces of furniture that you sleep in

**Try It**

**1.** Write a sentence using the plural form of one of these words: *peach, watch, wish, bush, dress, class,* or *box.*

_____

**2.** Write a sentence using the plural form of any word. Circle the plural word.

_____

# Lesson 3.12 Irregular Plurals

Some plural words do not follow the rules. Instead of adding an ending to these words, you need to remember their plural forms.

one *man*, seven *men*      one *foot*, two *feet*

one *woman*, five *women*      one *goose*, ten *geese*

one *ox*, six *oxen*      one *child*, a lot of *children*

one *mouse*, many *mice*      one *die*, two *dice*

Some words do not change at all. The singular and plural forms are the same.

one *deer*, six *deer*      one *fish*, forty *fish*

one *moose*, two *moose*      one *sheep*, a dozen *sheep*

one *trout*, five *trout*      one *series*, three *series*

one *species*, nine *species*

**Match It**

Match each phrase below to the correct plural form. Write the letter on the line.

1. _____ one woman    **a.** fifty womans    **b.** fifty women

2. _____ one die    **a.** six dice    **b.** six dies

3. _____ a moose    **a.** many moose    **b.** many mooses

4. _____ the trout    **a.** hundreds of trout    **b.** hundreds of trouts

5. _____ one species    **a.** eight species    **b.** eight specieses

6. _____ the goose    **a.** four gooses    **b.** four geese

7. _____ one ox    **a.** a herd of oxes    **b.** a herd of oxen

8. _____ a child    **a.** most childs    **b.** most children

# Lesson 3.12 Irregular Plurals

## Solve It

On the lines below, write the plural form of each word in the box.

| | | |
|---|---|---|
| foot _____ | ox _____ | deer _____ |
| man _____ | mouse _____ | sheep _____ |

Use the words in the box to complete the rhymes below.

1. The room was filled with 25 _____, and every single man's name was Ken.

2. "Hurry, hurry, hurry!" said all of the _____. "Walking's too slow, let's take the jeep!"

3. I am only one tiny gray _____, and yet there are dozens of cats in this house.

4. Please do me a favor and move your _____. I do not want footprints all over my seat!

5. In the garden I see dozens of _____, and they've eaten all of my lettuce, I fear.

6. The man scratched his head and looked at the _____. "Was it you who ate my bagel and lox?"

7. If I've told you once, I've told you twice. There's no room in this house for any more _____!

## Try It

On the lines below, make up two of your own rhymes using one of the plurals from the exercise above.

1. _____

2. _____

## Lesson 3.13 Singular Possessives

When something belongs to a person or thing, they *possess* it. An apostrophe (') and the letter **s** at the end of a word show that the person or thing is the owner in a **possessive**.

| | |
|---|---|
| Julianne**'s** violin | the school**'s** gym |
| Ichiro**'s** basketball | the tiger**'s** stripes |
| the park**'s** gates | Trent**'s** sister |

**Proof It**

The possessives below are missing apostrophes. To add an apostrophe, use this symbol (v̌).

1. The White Houses address is 1600 Pennsylvania Avenue.

2. Two fires almost destroyed the home of the nations president.

3. The Presidents House, the Presidents Palace, and the Executive Mansion were early names for the White House.

4. The Oval Offices shape was chosen by President Taft.

5. Some of the worlds best artists have work displayed in the White House.

6. President Bushs dogs, Barney and Miss Beazley, are Scottish terriers.

## Lesson 3.13 Singular Possessives

**Rewrite It**

Rewrite the sentences below. Replace the underlined words in each sentence with a possessive.

Example: <u>The capital of Hawaii</u> is Honolulu.

   <u>Hawaii's capital is Honolulu.</u>

1. <u>The hometown of Ronald Reagan</u> is Tampico, Illinois.

   _____

2. <u>The nickname of Benjamin Harrison</u> was "Little Ben."

   _____

3. Theodore Roosevelt was <u>the youngest president of the nation</u>.

   _____

4. Laura Bush, <u>the wife of the president</u>, used to be a teacher.

   _____

5. <u>The 39th president of America</u> was Jimmy Carter.

   _____

6. Before he became president, one of <u>the jobs of Harry Truman</u> was farming.

   _____

**Try It**

Write a sentence about a well-known figure from history. Use a possessive in your sentence.

_____

_____

# Lesson 3.14 Plural Possessives

To form the **possessive of a plural** word that ends in **s**, add an apostrophe after the **s**.

the girls' room                    the monkeys' food
the berries' juice                 the teachers' decision

For plural words that do not end in **s**, add an apostrophe and an **s** to form the possessive.

the people**'s** goals              the men**'s** clothes

## Complete It

Read each sentence below. Replace the words in parentheses ( ) with a possessive. Write the possessive in the space.

1. (The thick white fur of polar bears) _____ keeps them warm during Arctic winters.

2. (The mother of the bear cubs) _____ protects her babies from wolves and other predators.

3. (The coats of caribous) _____ change colors, depending on the seasons.

4. (The flippers of seals) _____ make them strong, speedy swimmers.

5. When the young girl listened quietly, she could hear (the songs of walruses) _____.

| Tip | Apostrophes are the key to telling the difference between a plural and a possessive. |  |
|---|---|---|
|  | **Plural** | **Possessive** |
|  | thousands of bugs | a bug's wings |
|  | several boys | the boys' clubhouse |
|  | four watermelons | the watermelon's seeds |

## Lesson 3.14 Plural Possessives

**Identify It**

Read each phrase below. If it is plural, write **PL** on the line. If it is plural possessive, write **PP**.

1. _____ the playful baby seals

2. _____ the igloos' walls

3. _____ the floating icebergs

4. _____ the Arctic rivers

5. _____ hundreds of salmon

6. _____ the puffins' brightly-colored beaks

7. _____ the explorers' route

8. _____ the people's warm clothing

**Try It**

Write two sentences that include plural words.

1. _____

2. _____

Now, write two sentences that use the possessive form of the plural words from above.

3. _____

4. _____

## Review   Regular and Irregular Plurals and Singular and Plural Possessives

To make many nouns **plural**, add **s**.

    book, book**s**         car, car**s**         color, color**s**

If a noun ends in **sh**, **ch**, **s**, or **x**, form the plural by adding **es**.

    pouch, pouch**es**     kiss, kiss**es**     dish, dish**es**

If a noun ends with a consonant and a **y**, drop the **y** and add **ies**.

    country, countr**ies**   duty, dut**ies**     party, part**ies**

Some irregular words don't follow these patterns.

    man, **men**         mouse, **mice**     child, **children**

The singular and plural forms of some words are the same. The words *deer, fish, moose, sheep, trout, series,* and *species* are the same in their singular and plural forms.

An apostrophe (**'**) and an **s** at the end of a word show that a person or a thing owns something else. These words are **possessives**.

    the jacket**'s** zipper   Eric**'s** keys     the school**'s** mascot

To form the possessive of a plural word that ends in **s**, add an apostrophe after the **s**.

    the cars**'** lights     the students**'** ideas   the babies**'** bottles

For plural words that do not end in **s**, add an apostrophe and an **s** to form the possessive.

    the geese**'s** feathers   the women**'s** friends   the children**'s** room

### Putting It Together

Read the singular words below. Choose the letter of the correct plural from each pair in parentheses ( ). Write the letter in the space.

1. _____ fox (**a.** foxs **b.** foxes)     2. _____ cherry (**a.** cherries **b.** cherrys)

3. _____ calf (**a.** calves **b.** calvs)     4. _____ boss (**a.** boss's **b.** bosses)

## Review   Regular and Irregular Plurals and Singular and Plural Possessives

Complete the sentences below with the possessive of the plural word in parentheses ( ).

1. The _____ many uses have made them a popular food in America. (peanuts)

2. The _____ name for this nutritious nut was *goober*. (Africans)

3. Long ago, a bug called the boll weevil threatened the cotton _____ living. (farmers)

4. Southern cotton fields were almost destroyed by these _____ hunger for cotton. (bugs)

5. George Washington Carver did some experiments. The _____ purpose was to find as many uses as possible for peanuts. (experiments)

6. The _____ success helped the farmers decide to plant peanuts instead of cotton. (products)

7. Today, peanut butter is many _____ favorite food. (children)

Rewrite the phrases below as possessives.

1. the ideas of George Washington Carver _____

2. the flavor of the peanuts _____

3. the flowers of the peanut seeds _____

4. the filling of the sandwiches _____

5. the roots of the plant _____

6. the shapes of the peanut shells _____

# Lesson 3.15 Subject and Object Pronouns

**Pronouns** are words that take the places of nouns and proper nouns.
**Subject pronouns** take the place of subjects in sentences. Some subject pronouns are *I, you, he, she, it, we,* and *they.*

| | |
|---|---|
| *Eduardo* likes to rollerblade. | *He* likes to rollerblade. |
| *The mall* was crowded. | *It* was crowded. |
| *Serena and Libby* were in the newspaper. | *They* were in the newspaper. |

**Object pronouns** often follow action words or words like *to, at, from, with,* and *of.* Some object pronouns are *me, you, him, her, it, us,* and *them.*

| | |
|---|---|
| The horse **jumped** the fence. | The horse **jumped** it. |
| Joey went **with** Mr. Simms. | Joey went **with** him. |
| I put the letter on top **of** the dresser. | |
| I put the letter on top **of** it. | |

## Identify It

Read the sentences below. Underline each pronoun. Write **SP** above it if it is a subject pronoun. Write **OP** above it if it is an object pronoun.

1. The librarian gave him the book.

2. Heather and Chase took the puppy with them.

3. It will be sunny and 65 degrees today.

4. The children sang the song to her.

5. I will ask the owner tomorrow.

6. Ngozi received all the information from you.

| Tip | When you are talking about yourself and another person, always put the other person before you.<br>Jaya and I    Lee and me    He and I |
|---|---|

# Lesson 3.15 Subject and Object Pronouns

**Proof It**

Read the sentences below. Cross out the incorrect pronouns. Then, use this symbol (^), and write the correct pronouns above them.

1. The students in Ms. Curry's class are going on a field trip. Them are going to the museum.

2. Ms. Curry told we that the museum is her favorite field trip.

3. The bus will leave at 8:30 in the morning. She will be parked in the school's west lot.

4. Casey and Allison will sit together. Them are best friends.

5. Ibrahim or Peter might sit with I.

6. The Goose Creek museum is not far away. It did not take we long to drive to him.

7. Michael forgot to bring his lunch. Ms. Curry gave he half of her sandwich and an apple.

8. Me loved seeing all the fossils.

**Try It**

1. Write a sentence using a subject pronoun. Circle the pronoun.

_____

2. Write a sentence using an object pronoun. Circle the pronoun.

_____

# Lesson 3.16 Comparative Adjectives

**Adjectives** can be used to compare people or things that are similar. Add **er** to an adjective to compare two things.

> "The medium chair is hard**er** than the small chair," said Little Red Riding Hood.

Add **est** to compare three or more things.

> Papa Bear's bed is soft. Mama Bear's bed is soft**er**. Baby Bear's bed is soft**est**.

For adjectives that end in **e**, just add **r** or **st**.

> nic**e**, nice**r**, nice**st**   clos**e**, close**r**, close**st**   gentl**e**, gentl**er**, gentl**est**

For adjectives that end in a consonant and a **y**, drop the **y** and add **ier** or **iest**.

> tin**y**, tin**ier**, tin**iest**   spic**y**, spic**ier**, spic**iest**   bus**y**, bus**ier**, bus**iest**

**Identify It**

Read the sentences below. Choose the correct adjective from the pair in parentheses, and circle it.

## 4th Annual Fitness Challenge a Success!

Here are the results from last week's Fitness Challenge.

- Brad Dexter and Ariela Vega were the (faster, fastest) sprinters.
- The (youngest, young) student to participate was six-year-old Emily Yu.
- Most students said the obstacle course this year was (hardest, harder) than the one last year.
- Everyone agreed that the (easyest, easiest) event was the beanbag toss.
- The weather was both (sunnyer, sunnier) and (coldest, colder) than last year.
- The (stranger, strangest) thing that happened all week was when the clown made a homerun at the kickball game. No one knows who was wearing the clown costume!
- The cafeteria was (busiest, busier) after the challenges than it usually is at lunchtime.
- Morgan Bonaventure won the award for (Greatest, Greater) Overall Performance.

## Lesson 3.16 Comparative Adjectives

**Complete It**

Read each sentence below. Complete it with the correct comparative form of the adjective in parentheses ( ).

1. I wish it had been _____ during the Kite Race. (windy)

2. The _____ cheers came at the end of the day when Principal Sneed did jumping jacks wearing a suit. (loud)

3. Micah is _____ than Jack, but Jack can sink more basketballs. (tall)

4. The _____ race was between Nadia and Kyle. (close)

5. It is much _____ to ride a bike wearing a helmet than to ride a bike without one. (safe)

6. This year's awards were even _____ than they have been in other years. (nice)

**Try It**

1. Write a sentence using a comparative adjective to compare two types of animals.

   _____

   _____

2. Write a sentence using a comparative adjective to compare two things that you can see from where you are sitting.

   _____

   _____

# Lesson 3.17 Comparative Adverbs

**Adverbs** can be used to make comparisons. Some adverbs follow the same rules that adjectives do. For most one-syllable adverbs, add **er** or **est** to make a comparison.

The boy in the blue shorts ran *faster* than I did.

Over the summer, Katherine grew *taller* than Jane.

To make a comparison using adverbs that end in **ly**, use the words *more* or *most*.

Aunt Peg read the book *more slowly* than Uncle Calvin.

My sister sang *most beautifully* of all the girls in her class.

## Complete It

Fill in the spaces in the chart with the correct adverbs. Remember that some comparative adverbs need to be used with the words *more* or *most*.

| | | |
|---|---|---|
| slowly | _____ | most slowly |
| fast | faster | _____ |
| skillfully | _____ | _____ |
| happily | more happily | _____ |
| _____ | more patiently | most patiently |
| _____ | _____ | latest |
| safely | _____ | most safely |
| playfully | _____ | _____ |

## Lesson 3.17 Comparative Adverbs

**Proof It**

Read the diary entry below. There are seven comparative adverb mistakes. Cross out each mistake. To add a word, use this symbol (^) and write the correct word above it.

Saturday, September 24

Dear Diary,

Today was the first day of Flannery's obedience class. We got there soonest than most of the other dogs and owners. Flannery sniffed and greeted the dogs as they arrived. She wagged her tail most cheerfully than any other dog.

The class leader helped everyone teach their dogs some basic commands. He laughed more harder than anyone when Flannery stole a treat out of his pocket. I'm sure he will hide them carefullier next time. The little dachshund standing next to us fetched more eagerly of all the dogs. She had short little legs, but she could run more fast than many of the bigger dogs. At the end of the class, Mom and I clapped most loudest of all the owners! Flannery will get her diploma in no time!

**Try It**

I. Write a sentence comparing two or more people or things. Use some form of the adverb *playfully*.

_____

# Review | Subject and Object Pronouns, Comparative Adjectives and Adverbs

**Subject pronouns** take the place of subjects in sentences. Some subject pronouns are *I, you, he, she, it, we,* and *they.*

> *Uncle John* bought a sandwich.  *He* bought a sandwich.
>
> *Craig and Steph* skated at the park.  *They* skated at the park.

**Object pronouns** often follow action words or words like *to, at, from, with,* and *of.* Some object pronouns are *me, you, him, her, it, us,* and *them.*

> Sid **told** *Frank* the tire was flat.  Sid **told** *him* the tire was flat.
>
> Leo gave the book **to** *the girls.*  Leo gave the book **to** *them.*

Use **comparative adjectives** to compare things that are similar. Add **er** to an adjective to compare two things. Add the ending **est** to compare three or more things. If the adjective ends in **e**, just add **r** or **st**.

> dark, dark**er**, dark**est**  neat, neat**er**, neat**est**  large, larg**er**, larg**est**

For adjectives that end in a consonant and a **y**, drop the **y** and add **ier** or **iest**.

> sill**y**, sill**ier**, sill**iest**  tin**y**, tin**ier**, tin**iest**  bus**y**, bus**ier**, bus**iest**

For most one-syllable adverbs, add **er** or **est** to make a **comparative adverb**. To make a comparison using adverbs that end in **ly**, use the words *more* or *most.*

> The plane quickly flew *higher.*
>
> This time, she whispered *more softly.*

## Putting It Together

Read the sentences below. Circle each pronoun. Write **SP** in the space if it is a subject pronoun. Write **OP** in the space if it is an object pronoun.

1. _____ Mom asked you to take out the trash.

2. _____ They completed the entire marathon.

3. _____ It is in the refrigerator.

4. _____ The e-mail is from her.

# Review | Subject and Object Pronouns, Comparative Adjectives and Adverbs

Read the paragraph below. Cross out the eight incorrect pronouns. Use this symbol (^), and write the correct pronouns above them.

Last week, an exchange student named Annette came to live with we. Her is from France. Mom is a French teacher, so her can talk to Annette without any problems. Dad is terrible with other languages. Him knows a little French, but it is hard to understand him. Annette gave he some tips, but it hasn't seemed to help yet. Annette is going to go to class with Mom. Mom's students can ask she about life in France. Them are only allowed to speak French to Annette, so it will be good practice for they.

Read each of the following sentences. The adjective or adverb in each sentence is in **bold** type. On the line below the sentence, write your own sentence. Use a comparative form of the same adjective or adverb.

Example: Max lifted the **heavy** boxes and put them in the moving truck.
　　　　　An elephant is heavier than a horse.

1. Nina placed three **soft** pillows on the bed.

_____

2. The turtle walked **slowly** to the pond.

_____

3. Rory **happily** waved to his parents.

_____

4. Will you show me how to make this **tasty** chili?

_____

# Lesson 3.18 Synonyms and Antonyms

**Synonyms** are words that have the same, or almost the same, meanings. Using synonyms in your writing can help you avoid using the same words over and over. They can make your writing more interesting.

|  |  |  |
|---|---|---|
| quick, fast | present, gift | sad, unhappy |
| close, near | jump, hop | tired, sleepy |

**Antonyms** are words that have opposite meanings.

|  |  |  |
|---|---|---|
| old, young | wide, narrow | true, false |
| never, always | funny, serious | smile, frown |

## Complete It

Read each sentence below. If the sentence is followed by the word *synonym*, write a synonym for the underlined word on the line. If it is followed by the word *antonym*, write an antonym for the underlined word.

1. The rocks in the walls of the Grand Canyon are millions of years <u>old</u>. (antonym) _____

2. Limestone is the <u>top</u> layer in the nine layers of rocks. (antonym)

   _____

3. The waters of the Colorado River formed the <u>enormous</u> canyon. (synonym) _____

4. Francisco Vásquez de Coronado led the <u>first</u> Europeans to see the canyon. (antonym) _____

5. Native Americans lived in the canyon <u>before</u> Europeans arrived. (antonym) _____

6. If you <u>yell</u> into the canyon, you will hear echoes of your voice. (synonym) _____

7. People <u>like</u> taking burro rides through the canyon. (synonym)

   _____

NAME

## Lesson 3.18 Synonyms and Antonyms

**Solve It**

Write a synonym from the box beside each word in numbers 1–5. Write an antonym from the box beside each word in numbers 6–10.

| difficult | wrong | destroy | sleepy | giggle |
|-----------|-------|---------|--------|--------|
| close | cheap | speak | loose | same |

1. laugh _____

2. wreck _____

3. talk _____

4. shut _____

5. tired _____

6. right _____

7. expensive _____

8. tight _____

9. easy _____

10. different _____

```
r  t  j  d  e  g  h  o  s  q  d
f  d  i  f  f  i  c  u  l  t  g
j  e  i  b  w  g  h  m  e  y  y
o  s  a  m  e  g  e  d  e  u  r
a  t  w  b  k  l  a  e  p  z  n
w  r  o  n  g  e  p  n  y  u  o
l  o  o  s  e  k  c  l  o  s  e
g  y  c  l  n  s  p  e  a  k  d
```

Now, find the words from the box in the word search puzzle. Circle each word you find. Words are written across and down.

**Try It**

1. Write a sentence using a synonym for *terrific*.

_____

2. Write a sentence using an antonym for *boring*.

_____

## Lesson 3.19 Homophones

**Homophones** are words that sound alike but have different spellings and meanings. Here are some examples of homophones.

Did you *hear* that noise?          The party is *here*.

Connor *knew* it would rain today.          I like your *new* haircut.

There is only *one* pancake left.          I *won* the raffle!

*Our* family is very large.          Pick Sam up in an *hour*.

*Your* mom speaks Spanish.          *You're* my best friend.

### Identify It

Read each sentence below. If the word in **bold** type is used correctly, make a check mark (✓) on the line. If it is not used correctly, write its homophone on the line.

1. _____ Mei **new** the best way to get from Seattle, Washington, to Portland, Oregon.

2. _____ We are meeting for lunch an **hour** before we go up in the Space Needle.

3. _____ **You're** sister said that it rains a lot in Seattle.

4. _____ The Seattle Mariners **won** the game on Friday night!

5. _____ **Hour** class is going on a field trip to Pike Place Market.

6. _____ Is **your** boat docked in Puget Sound?

7. _____ The 1962 World's Fair was held **hear** in Seattle.

8. _____ The **knew** Seattle Central Library is a beautiful glass and steel building located downtown.

# Lesson 3.19 Homophones

**Complete It**

Read the following sentences. Complete each sentence with a word from the pair of homophones in parentheses. Write the word on the line.

1. Jada _____ they would take the Washington State Ferry to Bainbridge Island. (knew, new)

2. _____ family moved to Seattle because Mom works with computers. (Hour, Our)

3. I can see the Cascade Mountains from _____! (hear, here)

4. I am excited that _____ going hiking at Mount Rainier this weekend. (your, you're)

5. _____ of Seattle's most famous residents is computer giant Bill Gates. (Won, One)

6. Brendan did not _____ the guide say that Smith Tower was Seattle's first skyscraper. (hear, here)

7. The Seattle Seahawks moved into their _____ football stadium in 2002. (new, knew)

8. Does _____ uncle still work at the Seattle Children's Museum? (you're, your)

**Try It**

On the lines below, write two sentences. Use the word *won* in the first sentence. Use the word *one* in the second sentence.

1. _____

2. _____

## Lesson 3.20 Multiple-Meaning Words

**Multiple-meaning words** are words that are spelled the same but have different meanings. Look at how the word is used in the sentence to figure out which meaning it has.

In the first sentence below, the word *trunk* means *an elephant's snout*. In the second sentence, it means *a sturdy box used for storage*.

> The elephant used its *trunk* to pick up the stick.
> Grandpa's old photos are stored in a *trunk* in the attic.

In the first sentence below, the word *fair* means *a carnival*. In the second sentence, it means *equal* or *just*.

> Jonah rode on a Ferris wheel at the county *fair*.
> It is not *fair* that I have to go to bed an hour earlier than Amanda.

**Find It**

The dictionary entry below shows two different meanings for the same word. Each meaning is a different part of speech. Use the dictionary entry to answer the questions below.

> **watch** *noun* a small device that is worn on the wrist and used to keep time
> *verb* to look at or follow with one's eyes

1. Mikayla's grandparents gave her a watch for her birthday.
   Which definition of *watch* is used in this sentence? _____
   **a.** the first definition          **b.** the second definition

2. Did you watch the movie you rented?
   Which definition of *watch* is used in this sentence? _____
   **a.** the first definition          **b.** the second definition

3. What part of speech is *watch* when it is used to mean *a device used to keep time*? _____
   **a.** a noun          **b.** a verb

## Lesson 3.20 Multiple-Meaning Words

**Match It**

Read each sentence below. Choose the definition that matches the way the word in **bold** type is used in the sentence. Write the letter of the definition on the line.

1. _____ If you don't hurry, you'll miss the **train**!
   **a.** to teach something by repeating it
   **b.** a line of cars that move together along a track

2. _____ Mark scored a **goal** in the second half of the game.
   **a.** something that people work hard to achieve
   **b.** a score in a game when a puck or ball is shot into a certain area

3. _____ Eloise is the **second** child in a family of four girls.
   **a.** number two; the one that comes after the first
   **b.** a moment in time; a small part of a minute

4. _____ We dropped pennies in the **well** and made a wish for each one.
   **a.** healthy; good
   **b.** a deep hole in the ground, used to get water or oil

5. _____ Gabrielle's piano teacher is **patient** when she makes mistakes.
   **a.** not easily irritated or annoyed
   **b.** someone who is getting medical treatment

**Try It**

1. Write a sentence using one of the multiple-meaning words from the exercise above (*train, goal, second, well, patient*).

   _____

2. Now, write a sentence using the other meaning of the word you chose.

   _____

# Review  Synonyms, Antonyms, Homophones, and Multiple-Meaning Words

**Synonyms** are words that have the same, or almost the same, meanings.

    shut, close    friend, pal    dad, father    grin, smile

**Antonyms** are words that have opposite meanings.

    win, lose    over, under    happy, sad    asleep, awake

**Homophones** are words that sound alike but have different spellings and meanings.

| | |
|---|---|
| My school has a *new* cafeteria. | Raisa *knew* him long ago. |
| May I have *one* cookie? | The Cavaliers *won* the game. |
| *Your* shirt matches your eyes. | I think *you're* very funny. |

Sometimes two words are spelled the same but have different meanings. These words are **multiple-meaning words**. Use the context of the sentence to figure out which meaning is being used.

    The *fly* landed on the food.    Will you drive or *fly* to Detroit?

## Putting It Together

Read the following paragraphs. There are six incorrect homophones. Cross them out, and write the correct homophones above them, using this symbol (^).

"I am glad your used to hiking in the mountains," said Omar. "People who are not used to being up so high get tired quickly," he added.

"It is really beautiful hear," said Nate. "I know we've been hiking for only won our. It feels like we're miles away from the rest of the world, though."

"I new you would like this hike," replied Omar. "My family comes here every year. I'm surprised we haven't one an award for Most Outdoorsy Family of the Year!"

# Review | Synonyms, Antonyms, Homophones, and Multiple-Meaning Words

Read each sentence below. Then, write your own sentence. If there is an **S** at the end of the sentence, use a synonym for the word in bold type. If there is an **A** at the end of the sentence, use an antonym.

**1.** This was the most **exciting** trip Omar and Nate had taken. **A**

_____

**2.** Nate sat on a rock **under** a tree to retie the laces on his boots. **S**

_____

**3.** Their stomachs were **empty**, but they wanted to hike until dusk. **A**

_____

**4.** Suddenly, Nate and Omar heard a **loud** roar. **A**

_____

**5.** Omar **grinned** when he saw the little boys in the bushes pretending to be bears. **S**

_____

Choose the sentence in which the word in **bold** type is used the same way as it is in the first sentence. Write the letter of your answer in the space.

**1.** _____ Saki swung the **bat** as hard as she could.
    **a.** Ted has a new baseball **bat**.     **b.** The **bat** ate a bug.

**2.** _____ The tree's **leaves** are changing color.
    **a.** Dad **leaves** at 8:00.     **b.** Aimee raked the **leaves**.

**3.** _____ Grandpa used the power **saw** to cut the wood.
    **a.** The **saw** is in the tool chest.     **b.** I **saw** you at the movies.

NAME _____

Before you start writing, you need to make a plan. **Brainstorming** is one way to come up with ideas. You may not use all of your ideas. Still, you will find the one or two great ideas you were looking for.

Sit down with a pen and a piece of paper. Make a list of things you know a lot about or would like to learn more about.

| | |
|---|---|
| life in the Sahara desert | Eiffel Tower |
| basketball | space shuttles |
| islands | being an artist |

Which topic is most interesting? Once you choose your topic, you can start learning more about it. You may need to go to the library. You may need to use the Internet. You may even need to interview someone.

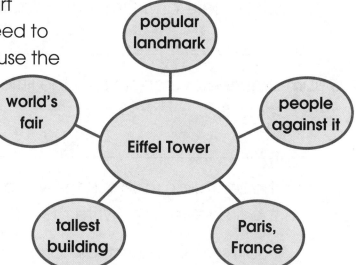

Once you have all your information, make an **idea web**. It can help you put your ideas in order before you start writing.

**Try It**

On a separate piece of paper, brainstorm your own list of ideas. Let your imagination go, and have fun! Choose the most interesting topic. If you need to, look for more information. Then, create an idea web.

## Lesson 4.2   Writer's Guide: Writing

When you first begin writing, do not worry about mistakes. You are just writing a **rough draft**. Look at the idea web you made when you were planning. Turn your ideas into sentences and paragraphs.

Do not worry about editing right now. After you have written your first draft, you can make changes and corrections. For now, just write. Here are some things to keep in mind as you write:

- Stay on topic.
- Include all the important details.
- Use complete sentences.

Here is an example of a rough draft. Can you see how the writer used the idea web to help write this paragraph?

> The Eiffel Tower is an intresting place to visit. It was built in Paris France. It was made for a world's fair The Louvre is a famous museum in Paris. The tower is very tall. It was the tallest building in the world many people did not think it should be built. it looks like they were wrong, though. Millions of people visit it every year! It is one of the most famus landmarks.

**Try It**

Use the idea web you made to write a rough draft on another piece of paper. Remember, this stage is all about writing, so write! You'll be able to edit your work later.

NAME _____

## Lesson 4.3  Writer's Guide: Revising

Now that you have finished writing, it is time to **revise**. Read what you have written. Sometimes it helps to read your work out loud. Ask yourself these questions:

- Do all of my sentences tell about the main idea?
- Can I add any details that make my writing more interesting?
- Are there any words or sentences that do not belong?

> The Eiffel tower is an intresting place to visit. It was built ^in *in 1889*
>
> Paris France. It was made for a world's fair. ~~The Louvre is a famous~~
>
> ~~museum in Paris.~~ The tower is ^~~very~~ tall. *986 feet* It was the tallest building in
>
> the world ^*for 41 years* many people did not think it should be built. ^it looks like *They thought it would be ugly.*
>
> they were wrong, though. ^*About 6* Millions people visit ~~it~~ ^every year! It is *the Eiffel tower*
>
> one of the most famus landmarks. ^*in the world*

In the paragraph above, the writer added some details. For example, explaining that the Eiffel Tower is very tall does not tell the reader much. It is more helpful to know that the Eiffel Tower is 986 feet tall.

The writer also took out a sentence that was not needed. The Louvre is in Paris, but it does not have anything to do with the Eiffel Tower. The writer decided that the sentence about the Louvre was not on topic.

### Try It
Look at all the changes the writer made. Can you see why each change was needed? Now, revise your rough draft. Doesn't it sound better already?

Spectrum Language Arts
Grade 3
138

Chapter 4 Lesson 3
Writer's Guide

## Lesson 4.4  Writer's Guide: Proofreading

**Proofreading** makes your writing stronger and clearer. Here are some things to ask yourself when you are proofreading:

- Do sentences and proper nouns start with a capital letter?
- Does each sentence end with a punctuation mark?
- Are any words misspelled? Use a dictionary if you are not sure.
- Are commas used in the right places?

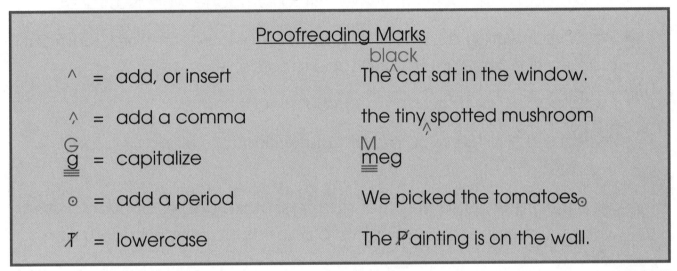

Proofreading Marks

| | | |
|---|---|---|
| ∧ | = add, or insert | The cat sat in the window. |
| ∧ | = add a comma | the tiny spotted mushroom |
| g | = capitalize | meg |
| ⊙ | = add a period | We picked the tomatoes. |
| ⫮ | = lowercase | The Painting is on the wall. |

The Eiffel Tower is an intresting place to visit. It was built in 1889 in Paris France. It was made for a world's fair. The tower is 986 feet tall. It was the tallest building in the world for 41 years many people did not think it should be built. They thought it would be ugly. it looks like they were wrong, though. About six Million people visit the Eiffel tower every year! It is one of the most famus landmarks in the world.

**Try It**

Use proofreading marks to edit your writing. Trade papers with a friend. It can be easier to spot mistakes in someone else's work.

## Lesson 4.5 Writer's Guide: Publishing

After all your changes have been made, write or type a final copy of your work. Your paper should look neat and clean. Now, you are ready to publish. **Publishing** is a way of sharing your writing with others. Here are some ways to publish your work:

- Read your writing to your family, your friends, or your classmates.

- Make a copy of your writing. Send it to someone who lives far away.

- Read your writing aloud. Have a teacher or parent record you. You can use a video camera or a tape recorder.

- Make copies, and give them to your friends.

- Ask an adult to help you e-mail your writing to a friend or a family member.

- Get together with some other students. Make copies of everyone's writing. Combine the copies into a booklet that each student can take home.

---

**From:** Tucker Boone
**Date:** May 20, 2014
**To:** auntlouisa@smileyhorse.net; grandpajoe@21stcentury.com
**Subject:** Eiffel Tower report

    The Eiffel Tower is an interesting place to visit. It was built in 1889 in Paris, France. It was made for a world's fair. The tower is 986 feet tall. It was the tallest building in the world for 41 years. Many people did not think it should be built. They thought it would be ugly. It looks like they were wrong, though. About six million people visit the Eiffel Tower every year! It is one of the most famous landmarks in the world.

---

**Try It**

Choose one of the ways listed above to share your work. What kinds of comments do your friends and family have? Can you think of any other ways to share your writing?

## Lesson 4.6 Writer's Guide: Writing a Paragraph

A **paragraph** is a group of sentences. Each paragraph is about one main idea. All the sentences tell more about the main idea. When you are ready to write about a new idea, start a new paragraph. When the paragraphs are put together, they make a letter, a story, or a report.

LA TOUR EIFFEL

A new paragraph does not start at the left edge of a piece of paper. It starts about five spaces from the edge. Leave an **indent**, or a space, about the size of the word **write**. This space tells the reader a new paragraph is starting.

The first sentence in a paragraph is the **topic sentence**. It tells what the paragraph will be mostly about. The next few sentences give more details about the topic. The last sentence is a **closing sentence**. It sums up the paragraph.

In the paragraph below, each important part is labeled.

**indent**          **topic sentence**

→ The Eiffel Tower is an interesting place to visit. It was built in 1889 in Paris, France. It was made for a world's fair. The tower is 986 feet tall. It was the tallest building in the world for 41 years. Many people did not think it should be built. They thought it would be ugly. It looks like they were wrong, though. About six million people visit the Eiffel Tower every year! It is one of the most famous landmarks in the world.          **closing sentence**

**details**

## Lesson 4.7  Writer's Guide: Writing a Friendly Letter

Writing a letter can be fun. It is exciting to open the mailbox and see a letter waiting. Writing letters can also be a good way to keep in touch with people who live far away.

Here are some things to keep in mind when you write a letter:

- **Write the date in the top right corner.** Remember to start the name of the month with a capital letter. Use a comma between the day and the year.
- **Begin your letter with a greeting.** Follow it with the person's name and a comma. Most letters begin with the word **Dear**.
- **Share some news in your letter.** What is new in your life? Have you done anything fun? Have you been someplace exciting?
- **Ask questions.** It is polite to ask how others are doing.
- **End your letter with a closing.** Some popular closings are **Sincerely**, **Yours truly**, **Love**, and **Your friend**. Use a capital letter to begin your closing. Use a comma after it.
- **Sign your name below the closing.**

May 20, 2014

Dear Grandma,

How are you? I am doing fine. Last week, I wrote a report about the Eiffel Tower. Mom helped me do some research on the Internet. I learned many interesting facts. For example, did you know that the Eiffel Tower has 1,665 steps? Mr. Strasser said my report was excellent. I told him that I plan to see the Eiffel Tower in person someday.

Please write back to me, and tell me what's new in Park City. I miss you a lot and hope you can visit soon.

Love,

Tucker

## Lesson 4.8   Writer's Guide: Writing to Convince

Have you ever tried to convince someone of something? To **convince** means **to get people to see things your way**. Maybe you have tried to convince your teacher that recess should be longer. Maybe you have tried to convince your parents to give you a later bedtime.

Words can be very powerful. You can change people's ideas with your words. Here are some tips for writing to convince:

- Think of all the reasons you feel a certain way. Make a list of your ideas.

- Now, think about why people might not agree with you. What could you say to change their minds? Add these ideas to your list.

- You are ready to begin writing. First, write a topic sentence about what you want or believe. Next, list your reasons. Finally, write a sentence that sums up your ideas.

| Eiffel Tower should be free | it's a public place |
| | more people might visit if free |
| | people could donate money |
| | money used to care for tower |

    People should not have to pay to visit the Eiffel Tower. The tower is like a park or a library. It belongs to everyone. People should be able to enjoy it at any time. Instead of paying to see it, people could donate money if they wanted to. This money could be used to take care of the tower. More people might visit the Eiffel Tower if they did not have to pay. It should be free for everyone to enjoy.

---

A **common noun** can be a person, place, or thing.

*teacher* (person)        *museum* (place)
*notebook* (thing)

A **proper noun** is a noun that names a specific person, place, or thing. Proper nouns are capitalized to show that they are important.

Here are some examples of common and proper nouns:

| Common Nouns | Proper Nouns |
| --- | --- |
| school | Hickory Hills Elementary School |
| zoo | Memphis Zoo |
| brother | Alexander |
| city | Tallahassee |
| day | Sunday |
| cat | Sasha |

**Complete It**

Complete the sentences below with a noun from the box. If there is a **P** after the space, use a proper noun. If there is a **C** after the space, use a common noun.

| Walnut High School | Saturday | town |
| dog | Jordan Lake | brother |

1. Uncle Dale is taking me fishing at ____Jordan Lake____ (P).

2. We will leave early on ____Saturday____ (P) morning.

3. My ____brother____ (C), Kris, is coming with us.

4. Uncle Dale lives an hour away in a __town__ (C) called Rockvale.

5. He is a math teacher at ____Walnut High School____ (P).

6. Uncle Dale's __dog__ (C), Patches, always comes fishing with us.

6

---

**Identify It**

Underline the nouns in the sentences below. The number in parentheses will tell you how many nouns there are. Above each noun, write **P** for *proper* or **C** for *common*.

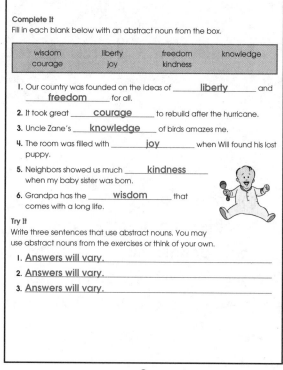

1. <u>Patches</u> jumped into the <u>rowboat</u>. (2)
   (P)                    (C)

2. <u>Kris</u> and I put on our life <u>jackets</u>. (2)
   (P)                         (C)

3. Last <u>August</u>, we went to <u>Griggs Lake</u>. (2)
        (P)              (P)

4. We stopped at <u>Elmwood Historic Car Museum</u> on the way <u>home</u>. (2)
                 (P)                                           (C)

5. We caught six <u>fish</u> on our <u>trip</u>. (2)
                 (C)          (C)

6. <u>Uncle Dale</u> cooked them on the <u>grill</u>. (2)
   (P)                                (C)

7. <u>Mom</u> made some <u>coleslaw</u> and <u>potatoes</u>. (3)
   (P)              (C)              (C)

**Try It**

1. Write a sentence using at least two common nouns. Circle the nouns.

   ____Answers will vary.____

   ____

2. Write a sentence using two proper nouns and one common noun. Circle the common noun. Underline the proper nouns.

   ____Answers will vary.____

   ____

7

---

**Abstract nouns** are nouns that you can't experience with your five senses. They are feelings, concepts, and ideas. Some examples are *friendship, childhood, bravery, hope,* and *pride.*

**Identify It**

Underline the abstract noun or nouns in each sentence below.

1. Maya's <u>honesty</u> is one of the reasons we are best friends.

2. Martin Luther King, Jr., wanted to change <u>hate</u> and <u>injustice</u> in the world.

3. Darius's <u>patriotism</u> is the reason he joined the army.

4. I love the <u>delight</u> on my sister's face on her birthday.

5. Your <u>kindness</u> will not be forgotten.

6. Benji felt great <u>pride</u> when his team won the championship.

7. What are your parents' best stories about their <u>childhood</u>?

8. It is important to me that you always tell the <u>truth</u>.

8

---

**Complete It**

Fill in each blank below with an abstract noun from the box.

| wisdom | liberty | freedom | knowledge |
| courage | joy | kindness | |

1. Our country was founded on the ideas of ____liberty____ and ____freedom____ for all.

2. It took great ____courage____ to rebuild after the hurricane.

3. Uncle Zane's ____knowledge____ of birds amazes me.

4. The room was filled with ____joy____ when Will found his lost puppy.

5. Neighbors showed us much ____kindness____ when my baby sister was born.

6. Grandpa has the ____wisdom____ that comes with a long life.

**Try It**

Write three sentences that use abstract nouns. You may use abstract nouns from the exercises or think of your own.

1. ____Answers will vary.____
2. ____Answers will vary.____
3. ____Answers will vary.____

9

---

A **pronoun** is a word that takes the place of a noun. Pronouns keep you from using the same noun or nouns over and over again.

Some pronouns take the place of a single person or thing: *I, me, you, he, she, him, her,* and *it.* Other pronouns take the place of plural nouns: *we, us, they,* and *them.*

In the examples below, pronouns take the place of the underlined nouns.

> The <u>grizzly bears</u> waded into the stream.
> *They* waded into the stream.
> <u>Molly</u> finished her report at noon.
> *She* finished her report at noon.
> Put <u>the bowl</u> on the table.
> Put *it* on the table.

**Identify It**
Read the paragraphs below. Circle each pronoun. You should find 15 pronouns.

Sonja Henie was an amazing figure skater. (She) was born in Oslo, Norway, in 1912. When Sonja was only five years old, (she) won (her) first skating contest. (It) was the start of a great career. (She) was a world champion for ten years. People around the world became interested in skating. (They) followed the career of the talented young girl.

Sonja also wanted to be a movie star. (She) moved to Hollywood and began acting. (She) also performed in a traveling ice show. (It) was very popular. Huge crowds came to watch Sonja perform. (They) could not get enough of (her.) Sonja enjoyed (her) fame and the money (it) brought (her.) But (her) first and greatest love was always skating.

**10**

**Rewrite It**
Read the sentences below. Rewrite each sentence using a pronoun in place of the underlined noun or nouns.

> Example: <u>David</u> kicked the ball toward the goal.
> *He* kicked the ball toward the goal.

1. <u>Bryan and Anna</u> had their first skating lesson on Tuesday.
   **They had their first skating lesson on Tuesday.**

2. <u>Bryan</u> had never skated before.
   **He had never skated before.**

3. <u>The ice</u> was slick and shiny.
   **It was slick and shiny.**

4. The teacher helped <u>Anna</u> tighten the skates.
   **The teacher helped her tighten the skates.**

5. The teacher told <u>Bryan and Anna</u> that they did a great job.
   **The teacher told them that they did a great job.**

**Try It**
1. Think about the first time you tried something new. Write a sentence about your experience. Circle the pronoun.
   **Answers will vary.**

2. Write a sentence using the pronoun *he, she,* or *it.*
   **Answers will vary.**

**11**

**Verbs** are often action words. They tell what happens in a sentence. Every sentence has a verb.

Ramon *put* on his running shoes. He *grabbed* his headphones. He *opened* the door and *took* a deep breath. Ramon *stretched* for a few minutes. Then, he *ran* down the street toward the park.

**Complete It**
A verb is missing from each sentence below. Complete the sentences with verbs from the box.

| breathed | moved | attached | invented |
|----------|-------|----------|----------|
| gave | kept | carried | helped |

1. In 1819, August Siebe ___**invented**___ the first diving suit.
2. The large helmet ___**attached**___ to a leather and canvas suit.
3. Weights ___**helped**___ divers stay underwater.
4. The divers underwater ___**breathed**___ air through hoses.
5. Later on, rubber suits ___**kept**___ divers dry.
6. The invention of scuba gear ___**gave**___ divers more freedom.
7. Divers ___**moved**___ from place to place on their own.
8. They ___**carried**___ their air with them.

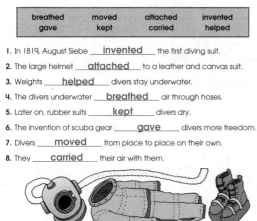

**12**

**Identify It**
Circle the 10 action verbs in the paragraphs below.

Jacques Cousteau (explored) many of Earth's oceans. In 1950, he (bought) a ship called *Calypso.* On the *Calypso,* Jacques (traveled) to bodies of water around the world. He (wrote) many books and (made) many movies about his travels. He (won) prizes for some of his work. Jacques also (invented) things, like an underwater camera and the first scuba equipment.

Jacques Cousteau (believed) it was important to protect ocean life. He (created) a group called the *Cousteau Society.* More than 300,000 people (belong) to the Cousteau Society today.

**Try It**
1. Write a sentence about a place you would like to visit one day. Circle the verb.
   **Answers will vary.**

2. Write a sentence about your favorite thing to do during the weekend. Circle the verb.
   **Answers will vary.**

**13**

A **linking verb** links the subject to the rest of the sentence. Linking verbs are not action words.

The verb *to be* is a linking verb. Some different forms of the verb *to be* are *is, am, are, was,* and *were.* Some other linking verbs are *become, feel,* and *seem.*

**Identify It**
Read the sentences below. Underline the linking verbs. Circle the action verbs. Some sentences may have more than one verb.

1. My grandmother is a marine biologist.
2. She studies undersea life.
3. She was always a good student.
4. She loved the ocean and animals as a child.
5. It was hard for her to become a scientist.
6. When she was young, some people felt women could not be good at science.
7. My grandma proved she was smart and hardworking.
8. One day, I might become a marine biologist myself.

14

---

**Solve It**
Use the linking verbs from the box to complete each sentence. Some may work for more than one sentence. Then, look for the linking verbs in the word search puzzle. Circle each word you find.

1. Today, my grandfather _____is_____ a stage actor.
2. He first __became__ a movie star at the age of 22.
3. He _____feels_____ lucky to have had such an amazing career.
4. I _____am_____ going to see him in a Broadway play next week.
5. When my dad _____was_____ little, he was in one of Grandpa's movies.

| feels | am | |
|-------|-----|--------|
| was | is | became |

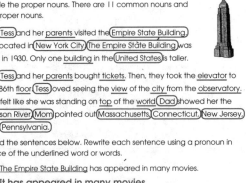

**Try It**
1. Write a sentence using a linking verb.
   **Answers will vary.**

2. Write a sentence using a linking verb and an action verb.
   **Answers will vary.**

15

---

**Nouns** name people, places, and things.
   *cousin   doctor   library   plant   sticker*

**Proper nouns** are capitalized. They name specific people, places, or things.
   *Aunt Claudia   Crestview Middle School   Rockefeller Center*

**Abstract nouns** are feelings, concepts, or ideas.
   *charity   hope   friendship   truth   trust   anger*

**Pronouns** can take the place of nouns in a sentence.
   *I   me   you   he   she   him   her   it   we   us   they   them*

Some **verbs** are action words. They tell what happens in a sentence.
   *read   fall   push   fold   laugh   stir*

**Linking verbs** link the subject of a sentence to the rest of the sentence.
   *is   am   are   was   were   become   feel   seem*

**Putting It Together**
In each sentence below, circle the verb. Write **L** in the space if it is a linking verb. Write **A** in the space if it is an action verb.

1. Taipei 101 is the tallest skyscraper in the world. __L__
2. Chicago's Home Insurance Building was the first skyscraper. __L__
3. Many TV stations broadcast from the Empire State Building. __A__
4. Large frames, not walls, support skyscrapers. __A__
5. In 1973, the Willis Tower became the tallest building in the world. __L__

Write two sentences using abstract nouns. Circle the abstract noun in each.

**Answers will vary.**

**Answers will vary.**

16

---

Read the paragraphs below. Underline the common nouns. Circle the proper nouns. There are 11 common nouns and 14 proper nouns.

Tess and her parents visited the Empire State Building. It is located in New York City. The Empire State Building was built in 1930. Only one building in the United States is taller.

Tess and her parents bought tickets. Then, they took the elevator to the 86th floor. Tess loved seeing the view of the city from the observatory. She felt like she was standing on top of the world. Dad showed her the Hudson River. Mom pointed out Massachusetts, Connecticut, New Jersey, and Pennsylvania.

Read the sentences below. Rewrite each sentence using a pronoun in place of the underlined word or words.

1. The Empire State Building has appeared in many movies.
   **It has appeared in many movies.**

2. Tess bought a postcard to send to her grandparents.
   **Tess bought a postcard to send to them.**

3. On their first date, Tess's parents went to the top of the Empire State Building.
   **On their first date, they went to the top of the Empire State Building.**

4. Tess learned that the building gets hit by lightning about 100 times per year.
   **She learned that the building gets hit by lightning about 100 times per year.**

17

---

# Answer Key

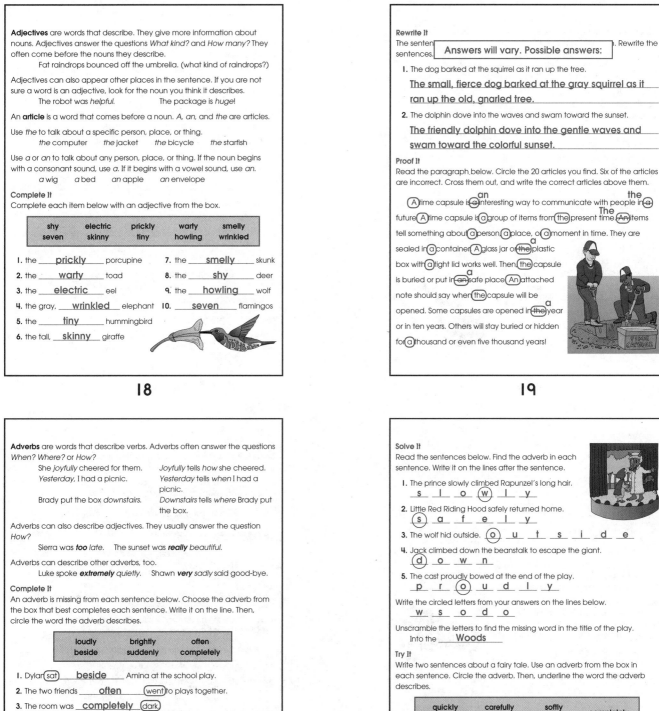

**Adjectives** are words that describe. They give more information about nouns. Adjectives answer the questions *What kind?* and *How many?* They often come before the nouns they describe.

Fat raindrops bounced off the umbrella. (what kind of raindrops?)

Adjectives can also appear other places in the sentence. If you are not sure a word is an adjective, look for the noun you think it describes.

The robot was *helpful.*          The package is *huge*!

An **article** is a word that comes before a noun. *A, an,* and *the* are articles.

Use *the* to talk about a specific person, place, or thing.

*the* computer      *the* jacket      *the* bicycle      *the* starfish

Use *a* or *an* to talk about any person, place, or thing. If the noun begins with a consonant sound, use *a*. If it begins with a vowel sound, use *an*.

*a* wig      *a* bed      *an* apple      *an* envelope

**Complete It**

Complete each item below with an adjective from the box.

| shy | electric | prickly | warty | smelly |
|-----|----------|---------|-------|--------|
| seven | skinny | tiny | howling | wrinkled |

1. the ___**prickly**___ porcupine
2. the ___**warty**___ toad
3. the ___**electric**___ eel
4. the gray, ___**wrinkled**___ elephant
5. the ___**tiny**___ hummingbird
6. the tall, ___**skinny**___ giraffe
7. the ___**smelly**___ skunk
8. the ___**shy**___ deer
9. the ___**howling**___ wolf
10. ___**seven**___ flamingos

**18**

**Rewrite It**

The senten[...]. Rewrite the sentences.

> **Answers will vary. Possible answers:**

1. The dog barked at the squirrel as it ran up the tree.

   **The small, fierce dog barked at the gray squirrel as it ran up the old, gnarled tree.**

2. The dolphin dove into the waves and swam toward the sunset.

   **The friendly dolphin dove into the gentle waves and swam toward the colorful sunset.**

**Proof It**

Read the paragraph below. Circle the 20 articles you find. Six of the articles are incorrect. Cross them out, and write the correct articles above them.

A time capsule is ~~a~~ *an* interesting way to communicate with people in ~~a~~ *the* future. A time capsule is a group of items from the present time. ~~An~~ *The* items tell something about a person, a place, or a moment in time. They are sealed in a container. A glass jar or ~~the~~ *a* plastic box with a tight lid works well. Then, the capsule is buried or put in ~~an~~ *a* safe place. An attached note should say when the capsule will be opened. Some capsules are opened in ~~the~~ *a* year or in ten years. Others will stay buried or hidden for a thousand or even five thousand years!

**19**

**Adverbs** are words that describe verbs. Adverbs often answer the questions *When? Where?* or *How?*

She *joyfully* cheered for them.      *Joyfully* tells *how* she cheered.
*Yesterday*, I had a picnic.      *Yesterday* tells *when* I had a picnic.
Brady put the box *downstairs.*      *Downstairs* tells *where* Brady put the box.

Adverbs can also describe adjectives. They usually answer the question *How?*

Sierra was **too** late.      The sunset was **really** beautiful.

Adverbs can describe other adverbs, too.

Luke spoke **extremely** quietly.      Shawn **very** sadly said good-bye.

**Complete It**

An adverb is missing from each sentence below. Choose the adverb from the box that best completes each sentence. Write it on the line. Then, circle the word the adverb describes.

| loudly | brightly | often |
|--------|----------|-------|
| beside | suddenly | completely |

1. Dylan (sat) ___**beside**___ Amina at the school play.
2. The two friends ___**often**___ (went) to plays together.
3. The room was ___**completely**___ (dark).
4. ___**Suddenly**___, the curtain (opened).
5. The scenery onstage was ___**brightly**___ (painted).
6. The children (said) their lines ___**loudly**___ so that everyone could hear them.

**20**

**Solve It**

Read the sentences below. Find the adverb in each sentence. Write it on the lines after the sentence.

1. The prince slowly climbed Rapunzel's long hair.
   s l **o** w l y
2. Little Red Riding Hood safely returned home.
   **s** a f e l y
3. The wolf hid outside.
   **o** u t s i d e
4. Jack climbed down the beanstalk to escape the giant.
   **d** o w n
5. The cast proudly bowed at the end of the play.
   p r **o** u d l y

Write the circled letters from your answers on the lines below.
w s o d o

Unscramble the letters to find the missing word in the title of the play.
Into the ___**Woods**___

**Try It**

Write two sentences about a fairy tale. Use an adverb from the box in each sentence. Circle the adverb. Then, underline the word the adverb describes.

| quickly | carefully | softly | |
|---------|-----------|--------|--------|
| suddenly | gently | sadly | completely |

1. **Answers will vary.**
2. **Answers will vary.**

**21**

# Answer Key

---

A **conjunction** joins together words, phrases, and parts of sentences. The most common conjunctions are *and, or,* and *but.* Other conjunctions are *since, because, although, if, while, unless,* and *however.*

      Chloe loves Brussels sprouts, *but* Haley won't eat them.
      *Since* you play soccer, can you give me some tips?

**Complete It**
Choose a conjunction to complete each sentence. Write it on the line.

1. Do you want to play the violin _____**or**_____ the piano? (or, but)

2. Mr. Randall canceled Lucy's lesson ____**because**____ he had a cold. (unless, because)

3. Let's play a duet at the recital _____**if**_____ we can learn it in time. (while, if)

4. Owen plays the drums, _____**and**_____ Marcus plays the trombone. (and, or)

5. Mrs. Klein likes to knit _____**while**_____ Ezra practices singing. (however, while)

6. Liam always practices his scales, _____**but**_____ Alla never does. (but, if)

7. Jade can buy a drum set, _____**however**_____ her parents want her to help pay for it. (however, or)

8. ____**Although**____ Vikram's lesson is at 11:00, he often arrives at 10:30. (While, Although)

**22**

---

**Rewrite It**
Combine each pair [ **Possible answers:** ] n. There may be more than one correct ans[     ]

1. Jack wants to take violin lessons. His sister has been taking them for years.

   **Jack wants to take violin lessons since his sister has been taking them for years.**

2. Nora plays piano by ear. She can't read notes at all.

   **Nora plays piano by ear, but she can't read notes at all.**

3. Dion enjoys listening to music. He doesn't play any instruments yet.

   **Although Dion enjoys listening to music, he doesn't play any instruments yet.**

4. Mr. Santiago hums. He practices every afternoon.

   **Mr. Santiago hums while he practices every afternoon.**

**Try It**
Write a short paragraph about music. Use at least four conjunctions, and circle them.

**Answers will vary. Conjunctions should be circled.**

**23**

---

**Adjectives** are words that describe nouns. They answer the questions *What kind?* and *How many?*

      The *blue* bicycle had *two shiny* handles and a *loud* bell.

**Adverbs** are words that describe verbs, adjectives, or other adverbs. Adverbs often answer the questions *When?, Where?,* or *How?*

      *Yesterday,* Chris left for Tokyo. (when)
      I heard a loud noise *outside.* (where)

*A, an,* and *the* are **articles.** Use *the* to talk about a specific person, place, or thing. Use *a* or *an* to talk about any person, place, or thing.

      *the* button       *a* mask

**Conjunctions** can join words, phrases, or sentences.

      Mac *and* I are coming for dinner.
      Jordan swims, *but* Milo would rather skate.

**Putting It Together**
Underline the adverb in each sentence below. Then, write *when, where,* or *how* in the space to show which question the adverb answers.

1. Carousels are <u>often</u> called *merry-go-rounds.* ____**when**____

2. A carousel is a platform that turns <u>slowly</u> in circles. ____**how**____

3. Carousels may have <u>first</u> been used 1,500 years ago. ____**when**____

4. As a horse moves <u>up</u>, a child may try to grab the brass ring. ____**where**____

**24**

---

Read the sentences below. If the underlined word is an adjective, write *adj.* above it. If it is an adverb, write *adv.* above it. If it is a conjunction, write *con.* above it.

              *adv.*
    Example: Sophie whispered <u>softly</u> to her little brother.

             *adj.*
1. Carousels were very <u>popular</u> in America from about 1885 until 1930.

  *adj.*                   *con.*
2. <u>Early</u> carousels were powered with a crank, <u>but</u> this took a lot of work.

           *adv.*        *con.*
3. Carousels were powered <u>later</u> with steam, <u>and</u> then electricity.

            *adv.*
4. Carousels could <u>often</u> be found at fairs and amusement parks.

  *con.*    *adj.*
5. <u>Although</u> <u>graceful</u> horses were the most famous, there were also giraffes, tigers, rabbits, and ostriches.

Read the following paragraph. Fill in each space with the article *a, an,* or *the.* Circle the nine adjectives you find.

    Today, I went to __the__ Bushnell Park Carousel in Hartford, Connecticut. It is __an__ extremely (old) carousel. It was built in 1914. I rode __a__ (beautiful) (gray) horse. It was a (jumper) horse and had __a__ (long) (flowing) mane. My (little) sister and my mom rode together in __a__ chariot. We listened to (cheerful) music from __the__ organ. Later, we had __a__ picnic in the park. It was __an__ (exciting) day!

**25**

---

# Answer Key

---

**Page 26:**

A **statement** is a sentence that begins with a capital letter and ends with a period. A statement gives information.

    **D**iego will be 13 in April.        **S**udan is a country in Africa.

**Commands** are sentences that tell you to do something. Commands also begin with a capital letter and end with a period.

    **U**se the bright blue marker.        **C**hop the onions.

> **Tip**
> Statements usually begin with a noun or a pronoun.
> Commands often begin with a verb.

**Complete It**

The statements below are missing periods. Add periods where they are needed. Circle each period you add so that it is easy to see.

                                              Monday, July 16

Dear Diary,

    On Saturday, Shi-Ann and I set up a lemonade stand⊙We made colorful signs to hang around the neighborhood⊙Dad helped us make cookies and chocolate pretzels⊙We wanted to make sure our customers would be thirsty⊙

    At the store, we bought a tablecloth, cups, and napkins⊙Dad let us borrow some money to use in our change box⊙Once we opened for business, we had tons of customers⊙Shi-Ann and I had to keep making fresh lemonade all day⊙

    We each made ten dollars from our lemonade stand⊙I had fun, but now I know that owning a business is a lot of work⊙

**26**

---

**Page 27:**

**Identify It**

Read the sentences below. If a sentence is a statement, write **S** in the space. If it is a command, write **C** in the space.

1. It is simple and fun to make your own lemonade. __S__

2. Ask an adult to cut ten lemons in half. __C__

3. Use a juicer to squeeze the juice from the lemons. __C__

4. Mix the lemon juice with six cups of water. __C__

5. The amount of sugar you add depends on how sweet you like your lemonade. __S__

6. I use one cup of sugar. __S__

7. Stir in the sugar until it dissolves. __C__

8. Add some ice, and enjoy a glass of cool, refreshing lemonade. __C__

**Try It**

1. Write a command you might use to advertise a lemonade stand. Remember, a command usually begins with a verb.

    Example: Buy some cold, sweet lemonade today.

    **Answers will vary.**

2. Write a statement about a business that you could start on your own.

    **Answers will vary.**

**27**

---

**Page 28:**

**Questions** are sentences that ask something. When a person asks a question, he or she is looking for information. A question begins with a capital letter and ends with a question mark.

    **W**ill you go to the party with me**?**
    **W**hat is the weather like in Phoenix**?**

**Rewrite It**

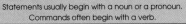

Answers will vary. Possible answers:

Example: It was cold and rainy on Saturday.
    __What was the weather like on Saturday?__

1. The largest frog in the world is called the Goliath frog.
    __What is the largest frog in the world?__

2. The skin of a toad feels dry and bumpy.
    __How does a toad's skin feel?__

3. Gliding leaf tree frogs can glide almost 50 feet in the air.
    __How far can gliding leaf tree frogs glide?__

4. The poison-dart frog lives in Colombia, South America.
    __Where does the poison-dart frog live?__

5. There are more than 4,000 species of frogs in the world.
    __How many species of frogs are there?__

> **Tip**
> Questions often begin with the words *who, what, where, when, how,* or *why.*

**28**

---

**Page 29:**

**Proof It**

Read the following paragraphs. There are seven incorrect end marks. Cross out the mistakes. Then, write the correct end marks above them.

    Have you ever heard someone say it was "raining frogs"**?** You might have thought that it was just a figure of speech. But in rare cases, it has actually rained frogs**⊙** How could this happen**?** It sounds impossible. During a tornado or a powerful thunderstorm, water from a pond or lake can be sucked into the air. This includes anything that is in the water.

    The storm continues to move**⊙** As it travels, it releases the water into the air. Does this mean that frogs and fish come raining down from the sky**?** Yes, this is exactly what happens.

    Cases of strange things falling from the sky have been reported for many years**⊙** People have seen small frogs, fish, grasshoppers, and snails drop from the sky in places like France, India, Louisiana, and Kansas. Are animals the only things that get swept up by storms**?** No. In fact, in 1995, it rained soda cans in the Midwest.

**Try It**

1. Write a question you would like to ask a frog expert.

    **Answers will vary.**

2. Write a question you would like to ask a weather expert.

    **Answers will vary.**

**29**

---

**Exclamations** are sentences that show excitement or surprise. Exclamations begin with a capital letter and end with an exclamation point.

> The Gold Nuggets won the championship!
> We missed the bus!

Sometimes an exclamation can be a single word. Sometimes it can contain a command.

> Oops!    Uh-oh!    Watch out!    Come back!

**Complete It**

Read the advertisement below. Some of the end marks are missing. Write the correct end marks on the lines.

**Kirby's Toy Store** is closing.

Get new toys while they last !

Prices are being slashed every day! Toys are 50%-75% off !

Our store is open every night until 9:00 .

We are located at the corner of Nelson Road and Ash Street .

Tell your friends ! Tell your neighbors !

**Don't miss out on the best toy sale of the year** !

30

---

**Proof It**

Read the sentences below. If the end mark is correct, make a check mark (✓) on the line. If the end mark is not correct, cross it out and write the correct end mark in the space.

1. Watch out ~~.~~ __!__
2. Did you take the dog for a walk ~~.~~ __?__
3. Luis is going to learn how to play the trumpet ~~!~~ __.__
4. We won the game ~~.~~ __!__
5. I lost my wallet ~~.~~ __!__
6. How old is Ella ~~.~~ __?__
7. My grandma had 16 brothers and sisters! __✓__
8. Harry wore a new suit to the wedding. __✓__

**Try It**

Imagine that you were going on a jungle animal safari. Think of two exclamations you might make. Write them on the lines below.

Examples: Watch out for that big snake!
> That leopard runs really fast!

**Answers will vary.**

31

---

All sentences begin with a capital letter and end with a punctuation mark.

**Statements** are sentences that give information. A statement ends with a period.

> About 3,000 languages are spoken in the world today.

**Commands** are sentences that tell you to do something. A command usually begins with a verb and ends with a period.

> Put away the games when you have finished playing.

**Questions** are sentences that request, or ask, for information. A question ends with a question mark.

> When will Mr. Belzer arrive?

**Exclamations** are sentences that show surprise or excitement. An exclamation ends with an exclamation point.

> I can't wait to meet the star of the show!

**Putting It Together**

Read the sentences below. Add the correct end mark. Then, write **S** if the sentence is a statement, **Q** if it is a question, **E** if it is an exclamation, or **C** if it is a command.

1. Have you ever heard of the Guinness World Records **?**  __Q__
2. My sister tried to break the record for fastest backwards speller **.**  __S__
3. Robert Wadlow, the tallest man, was 8 feet 11 inches tall **!**  __E__
4. A dog named Olive Oyl set the record for jumping rope **.**  __S__
5. What kind of evidence do you need to show that you have broken a record **?**  __Q__
6. Susan Williams blew a bubble larger than a basketball **!**  __E__
7. Practice hard, and you may set a record one day **.**  __C__

32

---

Read the newspaper article below. There are eight mistakes in end punctuation. Cross out the incorrect end marks, and add the correct ones.

## Flying Fossett Sets Another Record

Steve Fossett is an interesting person who loves adventure **.** He has set many records. For example, in 1997, he flew around the world in a hot air balloon **.** In March of 2005, Steve broke another record. He flew solo around the world in an airplane without stopping. This flight took him more than 67 hours **!** Can you imagine sitting in a plane for that long **?**

Steve's plane weighed about 22,000 pounds. More than 18,000 pounds of the weight was fuel **.** Steve needed to be sure there would be enough fuel for the trip **.** For a while, it looked as though he might not have enough fuel. But Steve kept going and safely landed in Kansas. What an amazing trip **!** What record do you think Steve Fossett will set next **?**

1. Answer the following question with a statement: Why do you think Steve Fossett has set so many records?

   **Answers will vary.**

2. If you could ask Steve one question, what would it be?

   **Answers will vary.**

3. Imagine that you were there when Steve finished his flight. Think of an exclamation you might say to him. Write it on the line.

   **Answers will vary.**

33

---

# Answer Key

The **subject** of a sentence is what a sentence is about. In a statement, the subject is usually found at the beginning of the sentence before the verb. A subject can be a single word or it can be several words.

*The entire team* cheered when the winning goal was scored.
*Irina* loves to eat oatmeal for breakfast.
*Brian Adams and Brian Rowley* are in the same class.
*Four raccoons, three chipmunks, and an opossum* live in my backyard.

## Identify It
Underline the subject in each sentence below.

1. The Golden Gate Bridge is located in San Francisco, California.
2. The bridge was built in 1937.
3. It was the longest suspension bridge in the world until 1964.
4. A suspension bridge is a bridge that hangs from cables.
5. Joseph Strauss was the engineer who designed the amazing bridge.
6. The Verrazano Narrows Bridge and the Mackinac Bridge are two other famous bridges.
7. The bridge's orange color was chosen so that it would be easy to see on foggy days.
8. Many movies and TV shows have included views of the bridge.
9. You can walk or bike across the Golden Gate Bridge during the day.

34

## Complete It
Each sentence below is missing a subject. Find the subject in the box that best fits each sentence. Write the subject on the line.

| The Golden Gate Bridge | A statue of Joseph B. Strauss |
|---|---|
| People and cars | Maria |
| The cost to build the bridge | About nine million people |

1. _____Maria_____ learned all about different kinds of bridges from her teacher.
2. __The Golden Gate Bridge__ is 1.7 miles long.
3. _A statue of Joseph B. Strauss_ celebrates the famous engineer.
4. __About nine million people__ visit the bridge every year.
5. _____People and cars_____ that travel north on the bridge do not have to pay a toll.
6. _The cost to build the bridge_ was 27 million dollars.

## Try It
1. Write a sentence in which the subject is a person's name. Underline the subject.

   Answers will vary.

2. Write a sentence in which the subject is more than one word. Underline the subject.

   Answers will vary.

35

A **predicate** tells what happens in a sentence. It tells what the subject is or does. The predicate always includes the verb. Finding the verb in a sentence can help you identify the predicate.

In the sentences below, the verbs are in bold type. The predicates are in italics.

Evelina ***recycles*** *all her cans and bottles.*
The seagull ***soared*** *above the stormy waters.*
Jermaine ***took*** *a picture of the dog with his camera.*

## Identify It
Read the paragraph below. Underline the predicate in each sentence.

In the United States, April 22 is Earth Day. On Earth Day, people celebrate the planet Earth. They take the time to remember that the environment is fragile. The first Earth Day was held in 1970. About 20 million Americans celebrated that year. Today, more than 500 million people around the world take part in Earth Day activities.

On Earth Day, people learn about different types of pollution. They also learn what they can do to help save the planet. Many people recycle things. Paper, glass, and aluminum can be reused in new ways. Some groups plant trees to help keep the air clean. Others pick up litter in their parks and neighborhoods. For some caring people, every day is Earth Day!

36

## Rewrite It
One box below is filled with subjects. One box is filled with predicates. Draw a line to match each subject to a predicate. Then, write the complete sentences on the lines below. (There is more than one correct way to match the subjects and predicates.)

| Subjects | Predicates |
|---|---|
| Roma and Patrick | held an Earth Day 5K Run. |
| Alexis | cleaned ___ McCoy Park. |
| Ms. Piazza | Answers will vary. ways to reuse newspapers. |
| My sister and I | donated ten dollars to a fund for endangered animals. |
| The students at Waxhill Elementary | planted eight small trees on Earth Day. |

1. _____
2. _____
3. _____ Answers will vary. _____
4. _____
5. _____

## Try It
Write two sentences about something you can do every day to protect the planet. Underline the predicate in each sentence.

Answers will vary.

37

A sentence is a group of words that contains a complete thought or idea. All sentences have a subject and a predicate. Part of a sentence, or an incomplete sentence, is called a **sentence fragment**. Sentence fragments cannot stand alone.

Examples: *Drove to the store.* (no subject)
*Because the sun.* (group of words)
*The girls on the porch.* (no predicate)

**Run-on sentences** are sentences that are too long. They are hard to follow, so they need to be split into two separate sentences. If the two sentences are about the same idea, they can be joined with a comma and a conjunction like *and* or *but.*

Clare likes cheese her brother Miles does not. (run-on)
Clare likes cheese. Her brother Miles does not. (split into two sentences)
Clare likes cheese, *but* her brother Miles does not. (combined with a comma and conjunction)

**Identify It**
Read each item below. If it is a complete sentence, write **C** on the line. If it is a sentence fragment, write **F** on the line.

1. __F__ Threw the ball.
2. __F__ After Madeline made a basket.
3. __C__ James scored a goal.
4. __F__ Cheered, clapped, and yelled.
5. __C__ The volleyball bounced off the net.

38

**Proof It**
Read the paragraphs below. There are four run-on sentences. Make a slash (/) where you would break the run-on sentences into two sentences.

Example: The clown wore enormous shoes / he had a large, red nose.

There are many different breeds of dogs/each one has a special personality. Basset hounds are often thought of as hunting dogs. They have long, floppy ears and wrinkly skin/they can be loyal, friendly, and stubborn. Some people think their droopy eyes are sweet/others think these hounds always look sad.

Cocker spaniels are good dogs for families. They are friendly and good with children/they have beautiful, long silky ears. Cocker spaniels are usually tan or black in color.

**Try It**
On a separate piece of paper, write two sentence fragments. Trade papers with a classmate. On the lines below, turn your classmate's fragments into complete sentences.

1. __Answers will vary.__
2. __Answers will vary.__

39

The **subject** of a sentence tells who or what a sentence is about. A subject can be a single word, or it can be several words.
*Simon* bought butter and eggs.
*The green jacket and the dark gray coat* are too big for me.

A **predicate** tells what the subject is or does. The predicate in a sentence always includes the verb.
The giant turtle *lay its eggs in the sand.*
The mountains *look blue on rainy days.*

A **sentence fragment** is an incomplete sentence. Words need to be added to make a fragment a complete sentence.
Locked the door. (fragment)
Jamie locked the door. (sentence)

**Run-on sentences** are sentences that are too long. They can be split into two separate sentences, or they can be joined with a comma and a conjunction like *and* or *but.*
Meg lives in the country she loves horses.
Meg lives in the country. She loves horses.
Meg lives in the country, *and* she loves horses.

**Putting It Together**
In each sentence below, underline the subject and circle the predicate.

1. Early American farmers (had many problems with their crops)
2. Insects, diseases, and bad weather (ruined many crops)
3. Crows (ate seeds and seedlings from the fields)
4. Farmers (invented scarecrows to keep birds away from their plants)
5. Native Americans (used a form of scarecrow to protect their fields, too)

40

Read each item below. If it is a fragment, write **F** on the line. If it is a run-on sentence, write **RO** on the line. If it is a complete sentence, write **C** on the line. Then, underline the subject, and circle the predicate.

1. __C__ Scarecrows (did not scare birds away for long)
2. __F__ Farmers had to.
3. __RO__ They used two poles for the body they stuffed the clothes with hay or leaves.
4. __F__ Painted faces on the scarecrows' heads.
5. __RO__ Men's clothes were usually used women's clothes were often saved for other uses.
6. __C__ The best scarecrows (wore bells or other objects that made noise)

Read each run-on sentence below. If it should be split into two separate sentences, make a slash (/) in between the sentences. If the sentences are part of the same idea, add a comma and the word *and* or *but.* Use this symbol (^) to add a comma and the word.

Example: George rode his bike ^*, but* Stephanie walked.

1. Enzo and Shelley made their own scarecrow/they named him Franklin.
2. They used Enzo's old overalls/Shelley's dad gave them a straw hat.
3. Shelley and Enzo planned to use an old mop for the body ^*, but* they could not find one.
4. Enzo's mom donated a flowerpot/Shelley and Enzo painted a face on it.
5. They put the scarecrow in the garden ^*, and* it scared away birds for a few days.

41

# Answer Key

Sometimes sentences that tell about the same thing can be combined. Then, the writer does not have to repeat words. Instead, the writer can combine two sentences into one by using the word *and*.

    Terrence likes popcorn.        Peter likes popcorn.
    Terrence *and* Peter like popcorn.

Because the subject (Terrence and Peter) is plural, the verb form has to change from *likes* to *like*.

In the example below, both sentences tell about what Jill read, so they can be combined.

    Jill read a new book.        Jill read a magazine.
    Jill read a new book *and* a magazine.

## Identify It

Read each pair of sentences below. If the sentences tell about the same thing and can be combined with the word *and*, make a check mark (✓) on the line. If they tell about different things and cannot be combined, make an **X** on the line.

1. __✓__ Snakes are reptiles. Lizards are reptiles.

2. __X__ Cheetahs are mammals. Toads are amphibians.

3. __✓__ The robin ate some berries. The robin ate a worm.

4. __✓__ Tarantulas are spiders. Black widows are spiders.

5. __X__ The dolphin swam beside its baby. The whale headed for deeper waters.

**42**

---

## Rewrite It

Combine each pair of sentences below into one sentence. Write the new sentence on the line.

1. Bobcats live in the mountains of Virginia.
Bears live in the mountains of Virginia.

   __Bobcats and bears live in the mountains of Virginia.__

2. The deer drinks from the stream. The coyote drinks from the stream.

   __The deer and the coyote drink from the stream.__

3. The airplane startled the rabbit. The airplane startled the owl.

   __The airplane startled the rabbit and the owl.__

4. It is rare to spot mountain lions. It is rare to spot bald eagles.

   __It is rare to spot mountain lions and bald eagles.__

5. Andy saw a deer at dusk. Andy saw a raccoon at dusk.

   __Andy saw a deer and a raccoon at dusk.__

## Try It

Write two sentences about wild animals you have seen. Then, combine your sentences into a single sentence.

Example: I saw a wild turkey. I saw a woodpecker.
            I saw a wild turkey and a woodpecker.

__Answers will vary.__

**43**

---

When two sentences tell about the same thing, they can sometimes be combined using the word *and*. The first two sentences below are about what Veronica did at breakfast, so they can be combined.

    Veronica ate some cereal. Veronica drank a glass of orange juice.
    Veronica ate some cereal *and* drank a glass of orange juice.

Some sentences can be combined using the word *or*. Use *or* if there are several choices about what might happen. In the example below, we do not know which choice Habib will make, so the word *or* is used.

    Habib might walk home. Habib might ride his bike home. Habib might run home.
    Habib might walk, ride his bike, *or* run home.

If you list several things in a row, place a comma after each one.

## Complete It

Read the sentences below. Fill in each blank with the missing word.

1. Grandpa spread out the tent. Grandpa hammered the stakes.

   Grandpa spread out the tent __and__ hammered the stakes.

2. Will might look for sticks. Will might cook dinner.

   Will might look for sticks __or__ cook dinner.

3. Will put the pillows in the tent. Will unrolled the sleeping bags.

   Will put the pillows in the tent __and__ unrolled the sleeping bags.

4. Grandpa and Will might make sandwiches. Grandpa and Will might grill hamburgers.

   Grandpa and Will might make sandwiches __or__ grill hamburgers.

**44**

---

## Rewrite It

Combine each set of sentences below into one sentence. Write the new sentence on the line.

1. Grandpa stacked the wood. Grandpa found the matches. Grandpa lit the fire.

   __Grandpa stacked the wood, found the matches, and lit the fire.__

2. Grandpa toasted a marshmallow. Grandpa placed it between two graham crackers.

   __Grandpa toasted a marshmallow and placed it between two graham crackers.__

3. Will read in the tent with a flashlight. Will finished his book.

   __Will read in the tent with a flashlight and finished his book.__

4. Grandpa and Will looked at the night sky. Grandpa and Will found the Big Dipper.

   __Grandpa and Will looked at the night sky and found the Big Dipper.__

5. Next summer, they might sail down the coast. Next summer, they might go fishing.

   __Next summer, they might sail down the coast or go fishing.__

## Try It

1. Write two sentences that tell about things you do in the morning. Use a different verb in each sentence.

   __Answers will vary.__

2. Now, combine the two sentences you wrote using the word *and*.

   __Answers will vary.__

**45**

---

Sometimes, sentences can be combined.
> The leaves are green. They are shiny. They are large.

The adjectives *green*, *shiny*, and *large* all describe *leaves*. The sentences can be combined into one by using the word *and*. Remember to use a comma after each adjective except the last.
> The leaves are green, shiny, *and* large.

In the example below, only a comma is needed to combine the two sentences. Both sentences describe the jacket.
> The red jacket is Amelia's favorite. The jacket is warm.
> The warm, red jacket is Amelia's favorite.

**Identify It**
Read each set of sentences below. If the adjectives describe the same thing, the sentences can be combined. Make a check mark (✓) on the line. If they describe different things, the sentences cannot be combined. Make an **X** on the line.

1. __✓__ The strawberries are red. They are juicy.
2. __X__ The lemons are tart. The lemonade is sweet.
3. __✓__ I like wild blueberries. I like fresh blueberries.
4. __✓__ The grapes are ripe. They are dark purple. They are plump.
5. __✓__ The fuzzy kiwi is on the table. It is round.
6. __X__ Oranges are tropical. Apples can be red, green, or yellow.

46

---

**Rewrite It**
Combine each set of sentences below into one sentence. Write the new sentence on the line.

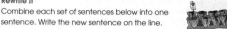

1. Cucumbers are long. They are thin. They are green.
   **Cucumbers are long, thin, and green.**
2. Sam grew some huge tomatoes in his garden. They were juicy.
   **Sam grew some huge, juicy tomatoes in his garden.**
3. The rabbits seem to love Mom's lettuce. It is leafy.
   **The rabbits seem to love Mom's leafy lettuce.**
4. The seedlings are tiny. The seedlings are pale green.
   **The seedlings are tiny and pale green.**
5. Rohan's peppers were small. They were spicy.
   **Rohan's peppers were small and spicy.**

**Try It**
1. Write two sentences that describe a piece of clothing you are wearing. Use a different adjective in each sentence.

   Example: I am wearing a new shirt. My shirt is striped.
   **Answers will vary.**

2. Now, write a sentence that combines the two sentences you wrote.

   Example: I am wearing a new, striped shirt.
   **Answers will vary.**

47

---

When sentences tell about the same thing, they can be combined. This helps the writer avoid repeating words. Commas and the words *and* and *or* are often used to combine sentences.

> Kirsten lives in San Diego.    Rafael lives in San Diego.
> Kirsten *and* Rafael live in San Diego.

> Bianca might take piano lessons.    Bianca might join a club.
> Bianca might take piano lessons *or* join a club.

> The popcorn is hot.   It is salty.   It is tasty.
> The hot, salty popcorn is tasty.   OR   The popcorn is hot, salty, *and* tasty.

**Putting It Together**
Read the sentences below. Fill in each blank with a comma or the missing word or words.

1. The Tangs went to the Mojave Desert. They went to Las Vegas. They went to Kelso Dunes.

   ___The Tangs___ went to the Mojave Desert _____,_____ Las Vegas, and Kelso Dunes.

2. The San Gabriel Mountains border the Mojave. The San Bernadino Mountains border the Mojave.

   The San Gabriel Mountains _____and_____ the San Bernadino Mountains _____border_____ the Mojave.

3. The world's largest thermometer is 135 feet tall. The thermometer is located in the Mojave.

   ___The world's largest thermometer___ is 135 feet tall _____and_____ is located in the Mojave.

48

---

Combine each set of sentences below into one sentence. Write the new sentence on the line.

1. Joshua trees live in the Mojave Desert. Joshua trees grow slowly.
   **Joshua trees live in the Mojave Desert and grow slowly.**
2. Joshua trees are found in California and Arizona. They are found in Utah. They are found in Nevada.
   **Joshua trees are found in California, Arizona, Utah, and Nevada.**
3. Native Americans made rope from the Mojave yucca plant. They made sandals and cloth from the Mojave yucca plant.
   **Native Americans made rope, sandals, and cloth from the Mojave yucca plant.**
4. July is very hot in the Mojave Desert. August is very hot in the Mojave Desert.
   **July and August are very hot in the Mojave Desert.**
5. The kit fox lives in deserts, on prairies, and on plains. The kit fox is small. It is gray.
   **The small, gray kit fox lives in deserts, on prairies, and on plains.**
6. The kit fox hunts at night. It eats small mammals.
   **The kit fox hunts at night and eats small mammals.**
7. Desert tortoises spend most of their lives underground. They can live for a year without water.
   **Desert tortoises spend most of their lives underground and can live for a year without water.**
8. Desert tortoises eat grasses. They eat wildflowers.
   **Desert tortoises eat grasses and wildflowers.**

49

---

# Answer Key

---

**Page 50**

The first word of a sentence always begins with a **capital letter**. A capital letter is a sign to the reader that a new sentence is starting.

*I* live on the third floor of the apartment building.
*Do* you like green beans?
*Here* comes the parade!
*Maya* grinned at Jeff.

**Proof It**
Read the paragraphs below. The first word of every sentence should be capitalized. To capitalize a letter, underline it three times (≡). Then, write the capital letter above it.

Example: <u>M</u>y sister taught me a new computer game.

<u>H</u>ave you ever played golf? <u>I</u>f you have, you know that it can be harder than it looks. <u>G</u>olfer Michelle Wie makes it look pretty easy. <u>T</u>hat's because she can hit a golf ball more than 300 yards! <u>A</u>t the age of 13, Michelle became the youngest winner ever of the Women's Amateur Public Links. <u>S</u>he has even played on the famous men's golf tour, the PGA Tour. <u>S</u>ome people think that this amazing six-foot-tall golfer will be the next Tiger Woods.

---

**Page 51**

**Rewrite It**
Rewrite each sentence below. Make sure your sentences begin with a capital letter.

1. michelle Wie's family is Korean.
   **Michelle Wie's family is Korean.**

2. she started beating her parents at golf when she was about eight.
   **She started beating her parents at golf when she was about eight.**

3. today, Michelle plays regularly on the LPGA Tour.
   **Today, Michelle plays regularly on the LPGA Tour.**

4. *competitive* and *determined* are two words that describe Michelle.
   ***Competitive*** **and** ***determined*** **are two words that describe Michelle.**

5. david Leadbetter was Michelle's coach for years.
   **David Leadbetter was Michelle's coach for years.**

6. what kind of golfing records will Michelle set in the future?
   **What kind of golfing records will Michelle set in the future?**

**Try It**
1. What sports do you like to play or watch? Begin your sentence with a capital letter.
   **Answers will vary.**

2. What sports figure do you most admire? Begin your sentence with a capital letter.
   **Answers will vary.**

---

**Page 52**

Capitalize the **specific names of people and pets**.
My cousin *Umeko* moved here from Japan.
We named the puppy *George*.

A **title** is a word that comes before a person's name. A title gives more information about who a person is. Titles that come before a name are capitalized.

*Grandpa* Bruce          *Aunt* Juliet
*Captain* Albrecht       *President* Abraham Lincoln
*Senator* Barbara Boxer  *Judge* Naser

**Titles of respect** are also capitalized.

*Mr.* Watterson    *Miss* Newton    *Mrs.* Cohen
*Dr.* Gupta        *Ms.* Liang

| Tip | If a title is not used with a name, it is not capitalized. My *aunt* is funny. The *judge* was here. But, if a title is used as a name, it is capitalized. Tell *Mom* I am going to the park. *Grandpa* will fix the computer. |
|---|---|

**Complete It**
Complete each sentence below with the words in parentheses ( ). Some of the words will need to be capitalized. Others will not.

1. Kelly took her dog, _____**Abby**_____, for a walk to the park. (abby)

2. My school has a new ____**principal**____. (principal)

3. On Tuesday, ____**Grandma**____ is coming to visit. (grandma)

4. The best teacher I ever had was ____**Mr. Butler**____. (mr. butler)

5. The baby dolphin at the zoo is named ____**Michi**____. (michi)

---

**Page 53**

**Proof It**
Read the letter below. There are ten mistakes. To capitalize a letter, underline it three times, and write the capital letter above it. To lowercase a letter (or change it from a capital letter to a small letter), make a slash through it. Then, write the small letter above it.

Example: Olivia and <u>m</u>att asked their <del>G</del>randma if she knew <u>mr</u>. Buckman.

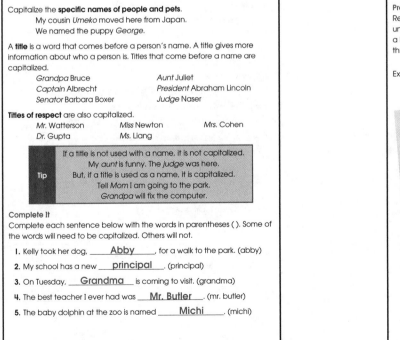

---

## Page 54

The **names of specific places** always begin with a capital letter.

| | |
|---|---|
| *Madison, Wisconsin* | *Rocky Mountains* |
| *Italy* | *Liberty Avenue* |
| *Science Museum of Minnesota* | *Jupiter* |
| *Jones Middle School* | *Los Angeles Public Library* |

**Complete It**

Complete each sentence below with the word or words in parentheses ( ).
Remember to capitalize the names of specific places.

1. There are many ___towns___ (towns) across ___America___ (america) that have interesting names.

2. Have you ever heard of Okay, ___Arkansas___ (arkansas)?

3. Some towns are named after foods, like Avocado, California, and ___Two Egg___ (two egg), Florida.

4. Some names, like Chickasawhatchee and ___Goochland___ (goochland) are fun to say.

5. A person from ___Russia___ (russia) might be surprised to find a town named Moscow in Vermont.

6. If you're on your way to visit ___Mount Rushmore___ (mount rushmore), look for Igloo, South Dakota.

7. Would you like to go to ___Boring Elementary School___ (boring elementary school) in Boring, Oregon?

| Tip | In the names of specific places, some words are not capitalized. All the important words begin with a capital letter. Small words, like *of, the, and,* and *a,* do not begin with a capital letter unless they are at the beginning of a sentence. |
|---|---|

**54**

## Page 55

**Proof It**

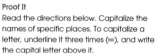

Read the directions below. Capitalize the names of specific places. To capitalize a letter, underline it three times (≡), and write the capital letter above it.

- Take wilbur street to preston parkway, and turn left.
- Travel about two miles on preston parkway.
- You will pass montgomery library and the talbot recreation center.
- At the light, turn right onto solomon road.
- You will drive over haystack bridge and pass a gas station.
- children's playhouse is located on the west side of the street.
- The address is 1548 solomon road.

**Try It**

On the lines below, write your own set of directions from your home to a friend's house. Be sure to include street names and any landmarks like schools, libraries, parks, and so on.

_____

_____

Answers will vary.

_____

**55**

## Page 56

The **days of the week** each begin with a capital letter.

Monday, Tuesday, Wednesday, Thursday, Friday, Saturday, Sunday

The **months of the year** are capitalized.

January, February, March, April, May, June, July,
August, September, October, November, December

The **names of holidays** are capitalized.

Memorial Day, Mother's Day,
Thanksgiving, Kwanzaa

**Complete It**

Complete the sentences below with the name of a day, month, or holiday. Remember to use capital letters where needed.

1. I was born in the month of ___Answers will vary.___

2. On ___New Year's Eve___, many people stay up until midnight to welcome the new year.

3. My favorite day of the week is ___Answers will vary.___

4. On ___Father's Day___, Austin made a card for his dad and washed his dad's car.

5. ___Wednesday___ is the middle of the week.

6. In northern states, it often snows in ___Answers will vary.___

7. The groundhog did not see his shadow on ___Groundhog Day___ this year.

8. Independence Day is on ___July___ 4th every year.

| Tip | The names of the seasons (*spring, summer, autumn,* and *winter*) are not capitalized unless they appear at the beginning of a sentence. |
|---|---|

**56**

## Page 57

**Rewrite It**

Rewrite the sentences below. Capitalize the names of days, months, and holidays.

1. presidents' day is on monday, february 21.

   ___Presidents' Day is on Monday, February 21.___

2. If the weather is nice, we will have a cookout on labor day.

   ___If the weather is nice, we will have a cookout on Labor Day.___

3. thanksgiving day always falls on a thursday.

   ___Thanksgiving Day always falls on a Thursday.___

4. Ty gave a valentine to every person in his class on valentine's day.

   ___Ty gave a valentine to every person in his class on Valentine's Day.___

5. Jessy is having a pool party on saturday, june 20.

   ___Jessy is having a pool party on Saturday, June 20.___

**Try It**

1. What is your favorite holiday? Why?

   ___Answers will vary.___

   _____

2. What is the coldest month of the year where you live? What is the warmest month?

   ___Answers will vary.___

   _____

**57**

## Page 58

The titles of books, movies, and songs are capitalized. Small words, like *of*, *the*, *and*, *in*, *to*, *a*, *an*, and *from*, do not begin with a capital letter unless they are the first or last word of a title.

| Books | Movies | Songs |
|-------|--------|-------|
| Stuart Little | Epic | "Down by the Bay" |
| Ramona the Brave | The Secret Garden | "Pop Goes the Weasel" |
| A Light in the Attic | Jumanji | "When You Wish Upon a Star" |

**Rewrite It**

Rewrite the sentences below. Capitalize the names of books, movies, and song titles.

1. It took Shakhil only two days to read the book how to eat fried worms.

   **It took Shakhil only two days to read the book How to Eat Fried Worms.**

2. Sara is sleeping over tonight, and we are going to watch toy story 2.

   **Sara is sleeping over tonight, and we are going to watch Toy Story 2.**

3. The song "let it go" is from the movie frozen.

   **The song "Let It Go" is from the movie Frozen.**

4. I love the poems in Bruce Lansky's book no more homework, no more tests.

   **I love the poems in Bruce Lansky's book No More Homework, No More Tests.**

5. Devon listened to the song "yellow submarine" on his mom's Beatles' CD.

   **Devon listened to the song "Yellow Submarine" on his mom's Beatles' CD.**

**58**

## Page 59

**Proof It**

Read the sentences below. There are 23 words that should begin with a capital letter but do not. To capitalize a letter, underline it three times. Then, write the capital letter above it.

1. I love to sing "hakuna matata" from the Lion King because the words are fun to say.
2. Have you seen the old version or the new version of The parent trap?
3. Felipe borrowed the way things work by David Macaulay from the library.
4. If you watch Schoolhouse Rock, you can learn the song "conjunction junction."
5. Last week, Lottie read Freckle juice and Chocolate fever.
6. madeline is the name of a book and a movie.
7. Reading the great kapok tree by Lynne Cherry is a good way to learn about rain forests.
8. My little sister sings "shake your sillies out" every morning.
9. Paul and Tyler saw walking with dinosaurs three times in the movie theater!

**Try It**

1. Imagine that you were shipwrecked on a desert island. If you could bring only one book with you, what would it be?

   **Answers will vary.**

2. What is the funniest movie you have seen in the last year?

   **Answers will vary.**

**59**

## Page 61

**Putting It Together**

Read the paragraph below. Find the nine mistakes in capitalization. To capitalize a letter, underline it three times. Then, write the capital letter above it.

saturday, july 7 was Lily's birthday. Lily and Mom decided that a movie marathon would be fun. Lily chose three movies to show at her party: Finding nemo, Hook, and the princess bride. Mom made popcorn balls. grandpa Henry made strawberry and chocolate ice-cream shakes. Lily could not wait for her friends Gabe, Tamiko, eliza, and Ben to arrive. she knew that her eighth birthday party was going to be a good one.

Complete each sentence below with the words in parentheses ( ). Some of the words will need to be capitalized. Others will not.

1. Tamiko's parents were born in ____Japan____. (japan)
2. Gabe's birthday is on ___New Year's Day___. (new year's day)
3. Lily's friends sang ___"Happy Birthday"___ when she blew out her candles. ("happy birthday")
4. Lily's ___grandma___ was born in 1947. (grandma)
5. Gabe and Eliza bought a birthday present for Lily on ___Thursday___. (thursday)
6. Lily loves to go to the ___movies___ with her mom. (movies)

**61**

## Page 62

A **period** is an end mark that follows a statement or a command.

    Put your bike in the garage.     Natalie has four brothers.

Periods are also used after initials. An **initial** is a letter that stands for a name.

    Darren *B*. Johnson    *P. L.* Travers    *J. P.* O'Bryan

The **days of the week** are often written as abbreviations, or in a shorter form. A period follows the abbreviation.

    Mon.  Tues.  Wed.  Thurs.  Fri.  Sat.  Sun.

The **months of the year** can also be abbreviated. May, June, and July are not abbreviated because their names are short.

    Jan.  Feb.  Mar.  Apr.  Aug.  Sept.  Oct.  Nov.  Dec.

**People's titles** are usually abbreviated when they come before a name.

    *Mrs.* = mistress  *Mr.* = mister  *Dr.* = doctor

**Types of streets** are written as abbreviations in addresses.

    *St.* = street  *Ave.* = avenue  *Dr.* = drive  *Ln.* = lane
    *Rd.* = road  *Blvd.* = boulevard  *Ct.* = court  *Cir.* = circle

**Match It**

Write the letter of the correct abbreviation on the line.

1. __a__ October 2      **a.** Oct. 2      **b.** Octob. 2
2. __b__ John Fitzgerald Kennedy      **a.** John F Kennedy      **b.** John F. Kennedy
3. __b__ Tuesday      **a.** Tu.      **b.** Tues.
4. __b__ Chester Avenue      **a.** Chester Avn.      **b.** Chester Ave.
5. __a__ December 19      **a.** Dec. 19      **b.** Dcmbr. 19
6. __b__ Madison Anne Hall      **a.** Madison A Hall      **b.** Madison A. Hall

**62**

## Page 63

**Proof It**

Read the schedule below. Cross out words that can be written as abbreviations. Write the correct abbreviations above them.

Mon. Mar.
~~Monday, March~~ 7

Thurs. Apr.
~~Thursday, April~~ 14

Fri. Apr.
~~Friday, April~~ 29

Sat.
~~Saturday,~~ May 21

Tues. Aug.
~~Tuesday, August~~ 30

Sun. Sept.
~~Sunday, September~~ 18

Hot Potatoes concert at 422
Dr.
Lakeshore ~~Drive~~—7:00

Cassie's dentist appointment with
Dr.
~~Doctor~~ Phillips—10:00

Mr.
Meeting with ~~Mister~~ Haddad—noon

Mrs.
Drop-off costumes at ~~Mistress~~ Jensen's
Ln.
house—1668 Dublin ~~Lane~~

Jimmy Ortega's birthday party—46
Blvd.
Brentwood ~~Boulevard~~

Mr.
Brunch with ~~Mister~~ Sato—11:00

**Try It**

1. Write a sentence about what you would do if someone gave you a hundred-dollar bill. End your sentence with a period.

Answers will vary.

2. Ask three friends when their birthdays are. Write the dates on the line using abbreviations for the names of the months.

Answers will vary.

**Tip**  Abbreviations for days, months, and types of streets are used only in addresses and casual writing. For example, you might abbreviate the name of a day or month in a calendar or a note. Do not use these abbreviations in the body of a letter, a report, or a story.

**63**

## Page 64

Use a **question mark** to end a sentence that asks a question.

Would you like some fruit punch**?**   How many books did you read**?**
Where is Connor going**?**   Can all birds fly**?**

**Complete It**

Read each an[    Answers will vary. Possible answers:    ]the answer.

Example: Q: How tall is Mr. Stein?
A: Mr. Stein is six feet tall.

1. Q: How many moons does Jupiter have?
A: Jupiter has at least 63 known moons.

2. Q: What is the largest body in the solar system?
A: The sun is the largest body in the solar system.

3. Q: Is Mars or Saturn closer to the sun?
A: Mars is closer to the sun than Saturn.

4. Q: When did Galileo make his first telescope?
A: Galileo made his first telescope in 1608.

5. Q: How long has Shannon Lucid spent in space?
A: Astronaut Shannon Lucid has spent more than 200 days in space.

6. Q: What is the smallest planet?
A: Mercury is the smallest planet.

**64**

## Page 65

**Proof It**

Read the paragraphs below. Cross out the six incorrect end marks. Add the correct end marks, and circle them.

Have you ever visited the Sleeping Bear Dunes⊙ They are located along the shore of Lake Michigan. The enormous dunes, or sand hills, are more than 400 feet tall in places. Many people travel to Michigan every year to climb the dunes⊙ Most visitors come in the summer, but some people come in the winter, instead. Why would they visit the icy shores of the lake in the winter⊙ Sledding down the steep slopes can be a lot of fun!

Do you know where the dunes got their name⊙ A Native American legend says that a mother bear lay on the beach to watch for her cubs after a fire. Over time, sand covered the bear⊙ Some people still think they can see the shape of a bear sleeping on the beach. This is how the dunes came to be called the Sleeping Bear Dunes⊙

**Try It**

On the lines below, write a question you could ask a park ranger at Sleeping Bear Dunes National Lakeshore.

Answers will vary.

**65**

## Page 66

An **exclamation point** is used to end a sentence that is exciting or expresses strong feeling. Sometimes exclamation points are used to show surprise or fear.

That pan is hot**!**   Lindsay won first-prize**!**
I can't believe you broke the chair**!**   There's a snake**!**

**Proof It**

Read the diary entry below. Five of the periods should be exclamation points. Find the five incorrect periods, and cross them out. Then, add exclamation points where they are needed.

Saturday, May 6

Dear Diary,

Something interesting happened today. I am going to be in a movie! The movie The Time Travelers is being filmed in my town. My mom works at the library. The director was learning about the history of the town at the library. My mom helped the director find what she needed. The director saw my picture on my mom's desk. She asked my mom if I would be interested in a small part in the movie. Would I ever!

I will have only two lines to say. Mom said she will help me memorize them. My scene will last about five minutes. Do you know what the best part is? I get to work with my favorite actor! I can't wait to start filming! Who knows? Maybe I'll be famous one day!

**66**

**67**

**Complete It**

The sentences below are missing end marks. Add the correct end mark in the space following each sentence. You should add four periods, two question marks, and three exclamation points.

1. Evan and Tanner have been jumping on the trampoline all morning **.**

2. Have you read the book <u>A Cricket in Times Square</u> **?**

3. Kazuki's swimming lesson was cancelled **.**

4. Watch out **!**

5. Please clean your room before bedtime **.**

6. The Bradview Tigers won the championship **!**

7. Would you like cheese on your sandwich **?**

8. There's a huge spider in my bed **!**

9. Tereza traded stickers with her little brother **.**

**Try It**

1. Write a sentence that shows excitement. Your sentence should end with an exclamation point.

   <u>Answers will vary.</u>

2. Write a sentence that shows fear. Your sentence should end with an exclamation point.

   <u>Answers will vary.</u>

---

**68**

A **period** is used at the end of a statement or a command.

   Reggie has a spelling test.        Stir the batter until it is smooth.

An **initial** is a letter, followed by a period, that stands for a name.

   James *K.* Polk     *A. L.* Wilhelm     Annette *P.* Desmond

The **days of the week** can be written as abbreviations.

   Mon.  Tues.  Wed.  Thurs.  Fri.  Sat.  Sun.

The **months of the year** can also be written as abbreviations.

   Jan.  Feb.  Mar.  Apr.  Aug.  Sept.  Oct.  Nov.  Dec.

**People's titles** are usually abbreviated when they come before a name.

   *Mrs.* = mistress   *Mr.* = mister   *Dr.* = doctor

**Types of streets** are abbreviated in addresses.

   *St.* = street   *Dr.* = drive   *Ln.* = lane   *Rd.* = road   *Ct.* = court

A **question mark** is used to end a sentence that asks a question.

   Are you feeling better**?**        What do penguins eat**?**

An **exclamation point** is used to end a sentence that shows excitement, strong feeling, surprise, or fear.

   My drawing won the contest**!**   Help**!**   This is the best party**!**

**Putting It Together**

Rewrite each item below using abbreviations wherever possible.

1. Saturday, November 4  <u>Sat., Nov. 4</u>

2. Doctor Khouri  <u>Dr. Khouri</u>

3. 1452 Winding Wood Lane  <u>1452 Winding Wood Ln.</u>

4. Mistress Bryson  <u>Mrs. Bryson</u>

5. John Paul Garrison  <u>J. P. Garrison or John P. Garrison</u>

---

**69**

Read the following paragraph. There are five incorrect end marks. Cross out the mistakes. Then, write the correct end marks above them.

When people go on vacation, they usually stay in a hotel or an inn. Some stay in cottages or cabins **.** Campers often sleep in tents **.** But have you ever heard of someone going on vacation and sleeping in a treehouse **?** If this sounds like fun, you might want to learn more about Out 'n' About Treesort. This unusual resort is located in Takilma, Oregon **.** There are 18 treehouses at Out 'n' About. There are also seven swinging bridges and five swings. Don't go there for a visit if you are afraid of heights **!**

Read the sentences below. If the end mark is correct, make a check mark (✓) in the space. If the end mark is not correct, cross it out and write the correct end mark on the line.

1. What kind of activities can kids do at Out 'n' About Treesort **?**

2. They can go horseback riding and rafting. **✓**

3. The highest part of the floating pirate ship is 52 feet from the ground **.**

4. Everyone is friends at the Treesort, and there are no locks on the doors **.**

5. Would your family enjoy sleeping in a treehouse? **✓**

---

**70**

Commas are used in dates. They are used in between the day and the year.

   March 4, 2006    September 22, 1750    June 1, 1991

Commas are also used in between the names of cities and states or cities and countries.

   Portland, Oregon    Paris, France    Minneapolis, Minnesota

When the names of cities and states (or countries) are in the middle of a sentence, a comma goes after the state or country, too.

   Bethany stopped in Burlington, Vermont, on her way home.

In an address, a comma is used between the city name and state abbreviation.

   Richmond, VA    Juneau, AK

**Proof It**

Read the sentences below. Add commas by using this symbol (∧).

Example: The Rock and Roll Hall of Fame is in Cleveland∧Ohio.

1. Basketball star LeBron James was born on December 30∧1984.

2. Sarah Hughes skated in the Winter Olympics in Salt Lake City∧Utah.

3. In 2004, Lance Armstrong traveled to Liege∧Belgium∧to ride in the Tour de France.

4. Olympic swimmer Michael Phelps was born in Baltimore∧Maryland∧ in 1985.

| Tip | When only a month and year are given, do not separate them with a comma. August 1999    February 2014    December 1941 |
|---|---|

## Page 71

**Identify It**

There are two choices below for each item. Choose the correct version, and write the letter in the space.

1. __b__ **a.** October, 12 1954    **b.** October 12, 1954
2. __a__ **a.** Omaha, NE    **b.** Omaha NE
3. __b__ **a.** August, 2007    **b.** August 2007
4. __a__ **a.** January 24, 1936    **b.** January, 24, 1936
5. __b__ **a.** Amarillo Texas    **b.** Amarillo, Texas
6. __a__ **a.** September 30, 2015    **b.** September 30 2015,
7. __a__ **a.** Nashville, Tennessee, is 284 miles from Shreveport, Louisiana.
       **b.** Nashville Tennessee, is 284 miles from Shreveport, Louisiana.
8. __a__ **a.** The ship traveled from Crete, Greece, to the shores of Turkey.
       **b.** The ship traveled from Crete, Greece to the shores of Turkey.

**Try It**

Ask two people in your class or your family the questions below. Record their answers on the lines.

1. In what city and state were you born?

   Answers will vary.

2. What is your birth date?

   Answers will vary.

**71**

## Page 72

A **series** is a list of words. Use a comma after each word in a series except the last word.

   Ms. Pinckney asked Alonzo, Erica, and Charley to work on the project together.
   Dakota put a sandwich, an apple, and a granola bar in her lunchbox.
   Our neighbors have two dogs, three cats, seven chickens, and a goat.

**Proof It**

Read the note below. Twelve commas are missing. Add commas where they are needed by using this symbol (∧).

Dear Dillon,

   Please go to the store for me when you get home from school. Tonight we are going to make muffins for Grandad's birthday breakfast. We will need blueberries, eggs, sugar, and lemon juice. I left some money on the kitchen table.

   Ellie is going swimming with Rob, Aliya, Eve, and Hunter. She will be home around 4:00. Please remind her to let the dog out, hang up her swimsuit, and start her homework.

   I made a list of the things you said you will need for your science project. I put glue, sand, newspaper, vinegar, and baking soda on the list. Is anything missing? We can go shopping tomorrow afternoon.

See you in a couple of hours!

Love,

Mom

**72**

## Page 73

**Rewrite It**

The numbered sentences are missing commas. Rewrite each numbered sentence in the recipe, using commas where needed.

### Lemony Blueberry Muffins

1½ cups flour
¼ cup yellow cornmeal
¼ cup sugar
1½ teaspoons baking powder
½ teaspoon baking soda
¼ teaspoon salt

½ cup milk
½ cup plain yogurt
3 tablespoons oil
1 tablespoon lemon juice
1 egg
1 cup blueberries

*Always have an adult help you when you are cooking.
- (1) You will also need cooking spray a muffin tin a measuring cup two bowls a teaspoon a tablespoon and a wooden spoon.
   You will also need cooking spray, a muffin tin, a measuring cup, two bowls, a teaspoon, a tablespoon, and a wooden spoon.
- Preheat the oven to 400°F. Spoon the flour into the measuring cup.
- (2) Combine the flour cornmeal sugar baking powder baking soda and salt.
   Combine the flour, cornmeal, sugar, baking powder, baking soda, and salt.
- (3) In the other bowl, combine the milk yogurt oil lemon juice and egg.
   In the other bowl, combine the milk, yogurt, oil, lemon juice, and egg.
- Add the wet mixture to the flour mixture. Stir until moist. Fold in the blueberries.
- Spoon the batter into the muffin tin. Bake at 400°F for 20 minutes.
- (4) Remove the muffins from the pan place them on a wire rack and let them cool.
   Remove the muffins from the pan, place them on a wire rack, and let them cool.

**73**

## Page 74

A **simple sentence** tells about one complete thought. A **compound sentence** is made of two or more simple sentences. To form a compound sentence, use a comma and the conjunction *and, or,* or *but* to join the simple sentences.

In the examples below, the underlined parts of each compound sentence can stand alone as simple sentences. Notice that a comma follows the first simple sentence.

   Sadie likes orange juice, *but* her brother prefers apple juice.
   Do you want to go to the zoo, *or* would you rather go to the art museum?
   Alejandro collects baseball cards, *and* Adam collects coins.

**Identify It**

Read each sentence below. If it is a simple sentence, write **S** on the line. If it is a compound sentence, write **C** on the line. Then, underline each simple sentence in the compound sentence.

1. __S__ Have you noticed birds in your yard or your neighborhood?
2. __C__ Feeding birds can be fun, and it can be educational.
3. __C__ Some birds like birdseed, but others like suet, a type of fat.
4. __S__ In the winter, many birds prefer fatty foods, like peanut butter.
5. __C__ Bird food placed on the ground will attract birds, but it will also attract other animals.
6. __S__ Squirrels are known for eating bird food and scaring birds away.
7. __S__ Once birds notice that you are feeding them, they will come to visit often.
8. __C__ Finches love thistle seed, and orioles love oranges.

**74**

# Answer Key

**Proof It**

Read the paragraph below. Three commas are missing from compound sentences. Add each comma by using this symbol (∧).

If you have a plastic soda bottle, you can make your own bird feeder. With an adult's help, make two holes on opposite sides of the bottle∧ and push a twig through each hole. Small birds can perch on the twig. Then, make several other holes in the bottle. The birds will be able to eat seeds from these holes. Tie some string around the neck of the bottle∧ and hang it from a sturdy tree branch. Enjoy watching the birds from a window∧ but don't forget to feed them.

**Try It**

1. Write a simple sentence about birds you have seen at a park or in your neighborhood.

    <u>Answers will vary.</u>

2. Write a compound sentence about other city wildlife you have seen.

    <u>Answers will vary.</u>

75

---

In dates, commas are placed in between the day of the month and the year. Do not use a comma between a month and a year.
    November 1, 1957    April 4, 2005    May 29, 1998    July 2000

**Commas** are also placed in between the names of cities and states or countries. When these names are in the middle of a sentence, a comma goes after the name of the state or country, too. In an address, a comma goes between the city name and state abbreviation.
    Wichita, Kansas    Syracuse, NY    London, England
    Takumi moved from Baltimore, Maryland, to Eugene, Oregon.

Place a comma after each word in a **series** except the last word.
    The soccer ball, football, and basketball are in the garage.

A **compound sentence** is made of two or more simple sentences joined with a comma and the word *and*, *or*, or *but*.
    Carla wanted to go to a movie, *but* Scott wanted to stay home.

**Putting It Together**

Read the paragraph below. It is missing seven commas. Add the commas where they are needed using this symbol (∧).

On May 14∧1804, a group of explorers left Saint Charles∧Missouri. Thomas Jefferson had hired Meriwether Lewis and William Clark to explore the American West. Jefferson wanted the group to learn about the land∧ the animals∧the plants∧and Native American tribes. The group followed the Missouri River west. They spent their first winter near a town that today is called Washburn∧North Dakota. A Native American woman named Sacagawea joined the group in November 1804. She was a helpful guide∧ but her greatest skill was as a translator.

76

---

Rewrite each sentence below. Add commas where they are needed.

1. Lewis and Clark met native people from the Oto the Blackfeet and the Sioux tribes.

    <u>Lewis and Clark met native people from the Oto, the</u>
    <u>Blackfeet, and the Sioux tribes.</u>

2. Jefferson hoped they would find water that connected the oceans but they did not.

    <u>Jefferson hoped they would find water that connected</u>
    <u>the oceans, but they did not.</u>

3. Hunters soldiers and boatmen made up much of Lewis and Clark's group of explorers.

    <u>Hunters, soldiers, and boatmen made up much of</u>
    <u>Lewis and Clark's group of explorers.</u>

4. The group returned to St. Louis Missouri on September 23 1806.

    <u>The group returned to St. Louis, Missouri, on September</u>
    <u>23, 1806.</u>

There are two choices below for each item. Choose the correct version, and write the letter on the line.

1. <u>a</u> **a.** August 1804        **b.** August, 1804

2. <u>a</u> **a.** November 4, 1804        **b.** November, 4 1804

3. <u>b</u> **a.** Portland ME        **b.** Portland, ME

77

---

The exact words a person says are called **dialogue**. One set of quotation marks is used before the first word of dialogue. A second set of quotation marks is used after the last word of dialogue.
    "I love to sail."                "Is the fruit ripe?"

If the dialogue does not end the sentence, put a comma (not a period) inside the quotation marks. The period belongs at the very end of the sentence.
    "I love to sail," Chloe said.        "The fruit isn't ripe," said Geoff.

If the dialogue is a question and does not end the sentence, keep the question mark inside the quotation marks.
    "Do you love sailing?" Chloe asked.
    "Are the bananas ripe?" asked Geoff.

If part of the sentence comes before the dialogue, put a comma after that part of the sentence. The period at the end of the sentence belongs inside the quotation marks.
    Chloe said, "I love to sail."        Geoff asked, "Is the fruit ripe?"

**Proof It**

Read each sentence below. If the sentence is correct, make a check mark on the line (✓). If it is not correct, make an **X** on the line. Then, use the proofreading marks in the box to show the changes.

| | |
|---|---|
| ∧ | = insert comma |
| ⊙ | = insert period |
| ∜ | = insert quotation marks |

Example: <u>X</u> ∜Our suitcases are in the attic∧" said Dad⊙

1. <u>X</u> ∜This summer, I am going to take Spanish lessons,∜ said Mackenzie.

2. <u>✓</u> "My family is driving all the way across the country in an RV," Ryan said.

3. <u>X</u> Nicolae said∧∜I plan to go swimming at the lake every day⊙∜

78

---

Spectrum Language Arts
Grade 3

# Answer Key

# Answer Key

---

Read the schedule below. Decide whether titles should be underlined or set in quotation marks. Then, mark them correctly.

**Schedule of Events for the Beaver River Kids' Center**

| | |
|---|---|
| August 4–10 | See the touching story of Sadako in the play <u>A Thousand Cranes</u>. |
| August 18 | Come to a special double-feature of the movies <u>A Little Princess</u> and <u>Because of Winn-Dixie</u>. |
| August 24 | Listen to Ian Nelson perform favorite poems like "Us Two" by A. A. Milne, "Someone's Toes Are in My Nose" by Bruce Lansky, and "Catch a Little Rhyme" by Eve Merriam. |
| September 4 | Meet famous author Ramona Darling. She'll be signing copies of her new book, <u>At the Top of the Cherry Tree</u>. |
| September 12 | Audition for the play <u>The Legend of Sleepy Hollow</u>. |
| September 23 | Come and listen to the band Foot-Stomping Blues perform favorite songs, like "No Time for Crying" and "Going to the Moon." |

Read each pair of sentences below. Choose the correct version of each sentence. Write its letter on the line.

1. __a__  a. Eli's book <u>Jake Drake, Bully Buster</u> is overdue at the library.
      b. Eli's book "Jake Drake, Bully Buster" is overdue at the library.

2. __b__  a. "Mom and I are going to the pool said Alicia."
      b. "Mom and I are going to the pool," said Alicia.

3. __b__  a. Aunt Daisy said. "Don't forget to bring the cupcakes with you,"
      b. Aunt Daisy said, "Don't forget to bring the cupcakes with you."

4. __a__  a. The story "The Adventures of Robin & Delilah" won first prize.
      b. The story <u>The Adventures of Robin & Delilah</u> won first prize.

**83**

---

The **subject** of a sentence tells who or what the sentence is about. When the subject is **singular**, it is only one person, place, or thing. When there is a singular subject, the verb ends with **s** or **es**.

Add **s** to most regular verbs that have a single subject.
   The boat sail**s** close to shore.      The woman water**s** the flower.

Add **es** to regular verbs that have a single subject and end in **sh, ch, s, x,** and **z**.

   Gran kiss**es** us good-bye.      Jake crunch**es** his cereal loudly.

When the subject is **plural**, it is more than one person, place, or thing. When the subject is plural, the verb does not end with **s** or **es**.
   The kittens sleep on the sofa.      Zared and Nina latch the gate.

**Proof It**
Read the paragraph below. Underline the subjects. Find the verbs that do not agree with their subjects. Add or delete s or es from the verbs so that they agree with their subjects. Use this symbol (^) to add a letter or letters. Cross out letters that don't belong.

<u>Mr. Ruskin</u> wash^es his historic car on Saturdays. <u>Aaron and Ali</u> help him. <u>Mr. Ruskin</u> sprays the old car with warm water. <u>He</u> scrub^s every inch of the car with a big sponge. <u>The children</u> polish^es the windshield and the mirrors. <u>They</u> use clean, soft rags. <u>Aaron</u> wax^es the beautiful red car. <u>It</u> shine^s in the sunlight. <u>He</u> wishes to have a car just like his dad's one day. <u>Mr. Ruskin</u> take^s Aaron and Ali for a drive in the shiny car every Saturday afternoon. <u>They</u> buy ice-cream cones. Then, <u>they</u> walk^s in the park.

**84**

---

**Complete It**
Read each sentence below. Then, read the pair of verbs in parentheses ( ). Choose the correct verb form. Write it on the line.

1. Emily and Mateo _____**toss**_____ a ball in the backyard. (toss, tosses)

2. The Jorgenson's _____**harvest**_____ their pumpkins every autumn. (harvest, harvests)

3. My little brother _____**brushes**_____ his teeth with an electric toothbrush. (brush, brushes)

4. Britta _____**bikes**_____ ten miles a day when she is in training for the race. (bike, bikes)

5. The blender _____**mixes**_____ the ingredients. (mix, mixes)

6. The Guzmans _____**camp**_____ near a crystal-clear mountain lake every summer. (camp, camps)

7. The shaggy Irish setter _____**catches**_____ the ball each time I throw it. (catch, catches)

8. Aunt Celeste _____**lives**_____ about two hours away. (live, lives)

**Try It**
1. Write a sentence using one of the following verbs: *climb, skate, twirl, travel, race, point,* or *bake.* Underline the subject in your sentence, and circle the verb. Make sure that the subject and the verb agree.

   **Answers will vary.**

2. Write a sentence using one of the following verbs *push, crash, finish, pitch, watch, miss,* or *fix.* Underline the subject in your sentence, and circle the verb. Make sure that the subject and the verb agree.

   **Answers will vary.**

**85**

---

*Am, is,* and *are* are all different forms of the verb *to be.*

*Am* is used only with the subject *I.*
   I **am** sleepy.      I **am** hungry.      I **am** under the bed.

*Is* is used when the subject is singular.
   Mickey **is** sixteen.      Annabelle **is** tall.      The beach **is** rocky.

*Are* is used with the subject *you.*
   You **are** very funny.      You **are** correct.      You **are** first in line.

*Are* is also used when the subject is plural.
   Haley Joel Osment and Dakota Fanning **are** actors.
   The boys **are** at home.

**Rewrite It**
Rewrite each sentence below. If it has a plural subject, rewrite it with a single subject. If it has a single subject, rewrite it with a plural subject. Remember that the form of the verb must agree with the subject and verb.

Example: The salad dressing and the salad are on the table.
   The salad dressing is on the table.

1. Nissa and Toby are eight.

   **Nissa is eight. OR Toby is eight.**

2. The photograph is in an album.

   **The photographs are in an album.**

3. The CDs on the shelf are from the library.

   **The CD on the shelf is from the library.**

4. We are excited about traveling to Mexico.

   **Answers will vary. I am excited about traveling to Mexico.**

**86**

---

Spectrum Language Arts
Grade 3

# Answer Key

---

## Page 87

**Proof It**

Read the paragraphs below. There are 11 mistakes with the verbs *am*, *is*, and *are*. Cross out each mistake. Then, write the correct form of the verb above it.

A topiary (*toe pee air ee*) ~~are~~ **is** a kind of sculpture made from plants. Topiaries ~~is~~ **are** cut to look like many different things. Some ~~am~~ **are** shaped like animals. For example, a topiary can look like an elephant, a bear, a horse, or even a dinosaur. Other topiaries ~~is~~ **are** trimmed to look like castles, cones, or mazes.

A topiary gardener ~~are~~ **is** an artist. He or she can turn simple shrubs into beautiful sculptures. Boxwood, holly, bay laurel, and yew ~~am~~ **are** some of the best plants to use for topiary. They ~~is~~ **are** easy to train and to trim.

In May, I ~~are~~ **am** going to visit the Green Animals Topiary Garden in Rhode Island. It ~~am~~ **is** one of the oldest topiary gardens in the country. There ~~am~~ **are** 80 pieces of topiary there! It ~~are~~ **is** fun to imagine all the green animals coming to life and roaming the gardens.

**Try It**

Write three sentences on the lines below. Use the verbs *am*, *is*, or *are* in each sentence.

Answers will vary.

**87**

---

## Page 88

*Has* and *have* are different forms of the verb *to have*.

*Have* is used when the subject is *I* or *you*.
I **have** a cold.          You **have** two brothers.

*Have* is also used with plural subjects.
We **have** a book about dinosaurs.
*Roberto and Chiara* **have** a baby sister.
*They* **have** a yellow house.          *Both cars* **have** flat tires.

*Has* is used when there is a single subject like *he*, *she*, or *it*.
*She* **has** blonde hair.          *The librarian* **has** a cheerful smile.
*A male deer* **has** antlers.

**Complete It**

Complete each sentence below with the word *has* or *have*. Write the correct word in the space.

1. Gus and Emily ___**have**___ a shell collection.

2. A horse conch ___**has**___ a cone shape and can grow to be almost two feet long.

3. Shells ___**have**___ value when they are beautiful or rare.

4. The shapes of some shells ___**have**___ interesting names, like helmet, basket, lamp, frog, and trumpet.

5. Oysters and clams ___**have**___ shells that are hinged at the back.

6. Emily ___**has**___ a necklace made from polished pieces of shell.

7. Cowrie shells ___**have**___ been used as money on Indian and Pacific islands.

8. If Gus ___**has**___ more than one of a certain shell, he will trade it with other collectors.

**88**

---

## Page 89

**Proof It**

Read the letter below. There are eight mistakes with the verbs *have* and *has*. Cross out each incorrect verb. Then, write the correct form of the verb above it.

August 6, 2015

Dear Kyra,

How is life at home in Massachusetts? We are having a great time in Florida. Gus and I ~~has~~ **have** 40 new shells to add to our collection! We ~~has~~ **have** been busy searching the beaches here. Gus and I already ~~has~~ **have** labels for our new shells. We don't want to forget their names by the time we get home.

Some shells still ~~has~~ **have** animals living in them. We never collect those shells. Our parents ~~has~~ **have** helped us look in rock crevices and tide pools. That is how we found a true tulip shell. It ~~have~~ **has** a pretty peachy color and an interesting pattern.

I ~~has~~ **have** a surprise to bring home for you. You ~~has~~ **have** never seen a shell like this. I can't wait to see you. Wish you were here!

Your friend,

Emily

**89**

---

## Page 91

**Putting It Together**

Read the paragraphs below. Cross out each incorrect verb. Then, write the correct form of the verb above it. You will find eight mistakes.

The Everglades cover about 4,000 square miles of land. They ~~is~~ **are** located in southwestern Florida. Marshes and swamps ~~makes~~ **make** up a large part of the Everglades. They are covered with saw grass. It ~~grow~~ **grows** to be about 15 feet tall. People cannot easily ~~reaches~~ **reach** much of the Everglades because the saw grass ~~am~~ **is** so thick. This area ~~are~~ **is** sometimes called *the river of grass*.

The Everglades have many different kinds of plants and wildlife. The tropical area makes a good home for birds like herons, egrets, spoonbills, and pelicans. The Everglades are the only place in the world that has both crocodiles and alligators. Deer, panthers, otters, and manatees ~~makes~~ **make** their homes there, too. Quiet visitors ~~catches~~ **catch** a glimpse of many animals.

Read each sentence below. Then, circle the verb from the pair in parentheses ( ) that best completes each sentence.

1. The black snake (hiss, (hisses)) at the nearby raptor.

2. Palms, pines, and cypresses ((grow,) grows) in the Everglades.

3. An alligator ((has,) have) a wide, flat snout, and a crocodile ((has,) have) a narrow snout.

4. The park ranger (watch, (watches)) people to make sure they stay safe.

5. Dragonflies ((gather,) gathers) their food while they fly.

**91**

---

Spectrum Language Arts
Grade 3

Answer Key

**164**

# Answer Key

---

Verbs in the **present tense** tell about things that are happening right now. Verbs in the **past tense** tell about things that have already happened.

Add **ed** to a regular verb to change it to the past tense. If the verb already ends in **e**, just add **d**.

The concert end**ed** at 9:00.　　　It snow**ed** 16 inches yesterday!
Uncle Donny taste**d** the pudding.　The waitress smil**ed** at the girl.

If a verb ends in **y**, change the **y** to **i** and add **ed**.

We hurry to catch the bus.　　We hurr**ied** to catch the bus.
I dry the laundry outside.　　I dr**ied** the laundry outside.

**Complete It**
Read the sentences below. Complete each sentence with the past tense of the verb in parentheses ( ).

1. Leonardo da Vinci ___painted___ the mysterious *Mona Lisa*. (paint)

2. Women and children often ___posed___ for artist Mary Cassatt. (pose)

3. The Impressionists ___showed___ the world that not all paintings had to look realistic. (show)

4. Grandma Moses ___loved___ to paint cheerful pictures of life in the country. (love)

5. Jackson Pollack, who made colorful paint-splattered paintings, ___studied___ with Thomas Hart Benton. (study)

6. Vincent van Gogh ___created___ more than 800 oil paintings during his lifetime! (create)

7. Chinese artist Wang Yani ___started___ painting when she was only two. (start)

**92**

---

**Rewrite It**
Read the sentences below. They are all in the present tense. Underline the verb in each sentence. Then, rewrite the sentences in the past tense.

1. Norman Rockwell lives from 1894 until 1978.

   **Norman Rockwell lived from 1894 until 1978.**

2. Norman studies at the National Academy of Design in New York.

   **Norman studied at the National Academy of Design in New York.**

3. He illustrates issues of children's magazines, like *Boys' Life*.

   **He illustrated issues of children's magazines, like *Boys' Life*.**

4. Norman paints scenes from everyday small town life.

   **Norman painted scenes from everyday small town life.**

5. Norman calls himself a storyteller.

   **Norman called himself a storyteller.**

6. A fire destroys many of Norman's paintings.

   **A fire destroyed many of Norman's paintings.**

7. Norman Rockwell receives the Presidential Medal of Freedom in 1976.

   **Norman Rockwell received the Presidential Medal of Freedom in 1976.**

**Try It**
1. Write a sentence in the present tense that describes a piece of art you have seen or made.

   **Answers will vary.**

2. Now, rewrite the same sentence in the past tense.

   **Answers will vary.**

**93**

---

Some verbs do not follow the pattern of regular verbs. The past tenses of these verbs are different. To form the past tense, do not add **ed** or **d** to these verbs. Instead, you must change the entire word.

| **Present Tense** | **Past Tense** |
|---|---|
| She *eats* a snack every day. | She *ate* a snack every day. |
| Mario *says* it will rain tonight. | Mario *said* it will rain tonight. |
| The tiny pine tree *grows* quickly. | The tiny pine tree *grew* quickly. |
| Catalina *makes* bracelets. | Catalina *made* bracelets. |
| I *ride* the bus downtown. | I *rode* the bus downtown. |

**Proof It**
Some of the verbs below are in the wrong tense. Cross out the verbs in bold type. Use this symbol (^), and write the correct word above it.

　　　　　　　　　　　　　　　　　　　　　said
When my mom was a little girl, her family owned a bakery. Mom ~~says~~ that she loved the sweet smell of bread and pastries baking in the ovens.
　　　　　　ate　　　　　　　　　　　　　　　　rode
Every morning, Mom ~~eats~~ a cinnamon roll for breakfast. She ~~rides~~ her bike to school when the weather was nice. In her bag, she carried fresh muffins for her teachers and her friends.
　　　　　　　　　　　　　　made
In the afternoon, she and her dad ~~make~~ crusty rolls and chewy bagels. Grandpa put all the ingredients in a big bowl. He and Mom took turns kneading the dough. Then, he covered it with a clean towel. The
　　　　grew　　　grew　　　said
dough ~~grows~~ and ~~grows~~. Mom ~~says~~ she loved to punch it down. Finally, she
　　　　　　　　ate
and Grandpa shaped the dough and popped it into the ovens.
　　　　　　　　ate
Mom's family ~~eats~~ fresh bread with dinner every night!

**94**

---

**Solve It**
Read each sentence below. On the line, write the past tense of the underlined verb.

1. Grandma always eats a blueberry bagel with cream cheese for breakfast. ___ate___

2. The Larsons say that Hot Cross Buns was the best bakery in town. ___said___

3. Mom's cousin, Eddie, rides his bike around town and delivered bread. ___rode___

4. Mom grows up helping her parents at the bakery. ___grew___

5. Every Saturday, Mom and Grandpa make 12 loaves of wheat bread, 15 loaves of French bread, and 100 dinner rolls. ___made___

| h | q | (s | a | i | d) | r |
|---|---|---|---|---|---|---|
| m | p | n | t | m | a | l |
| z | (g | r | e | w) | g | k |
| u | d | k | y | f | l | g |
| j | h | v | (r | u | a | e |
| i | b | b | o | w | d | y |
| t | (m | a | d | e) | x | c |
| j | s | f | e | (p | p) | e |

Now, find each past-tense verb in the word search puzzle. Circle the words you find. Words are written across and down.

**Try It**
1. What did you eat for dinner last night? Use a complete sentence to answer the question.

   **Answers will vary.**

2. Write a sentence that uses the past tense of one of these words: *say, grow, make,* or *ride*.

   **Answers will vary.**

**95**

---

Spectrum Language Arts
Grade 3

The past tenses of some verbs do not follow the patterns of regular verbs. To form the past tense, do not add **ed** or **d**. Instead, you must change the entire word.

| Present Tense | Past Tense |
| --- | --- |
| Franklin *gives* her an orange. | Franklin *gave* her an orange. |
| The goose *flies* over the pond. | The goose *flew* over the pond. |
| Marisa *brings* some games. | Marisa *brought* some games. |
| Beth *thinks* she got an A. | Beth *thought* she got an A. |
| I *write* a letter to my grandma. | I *wrote* a letter to my grandma. |

**Rewrite It**

The sentences below are all in the present tense. Rewrite them in the past tense.

1. Ms. Lucetta gives the class an assignment.

   Ms. Lucetta gave the class an assignment.

2. Nicholas and Liv write a play about a giant who lives in the forest.

   Nicholas and Liv wrote a play about a giant who lives in the forest.

3. They think the giant should be kind, not scary.

   They thought the giant should be kind, not scary.

4. A small bluebird flies many miles to save the kind giant.

   A small bluebird flew many miles to save the kind giant.

5. The bluebird brings him an important message.

   The bluebird brought him an important message.

6. The giant gives the bluebird shelter in his cave.

   The giant gave the bluebird shelter in his cave.

96

---

**Proof It**

Some of the verbs below are in the wrong tense. Cross out the underlined verbs. Use this symbol (^), and write the correct past-tense verbs above them.

Pradeep and Kent ~~write~~ wrote a play for Ms. Lucetta's class. Their play was about a brother and sister who ~~think~~ thought that an alien spaceship landed near their house. They named the brother and sister Harry and Carrie. In the play, something very large ~~flies~~ flew over Harry and Carrie's house one night. It made a loud whirring noise. Its lights flashed on and off.

Carrie ran to the window. She ~~think~~ thought it was a helicopter until she saw how big it was. Harry ran into the backyard. He ~~brings~~ brought his camera with him. Harry took as many photos as he could. Then, the ship grew silent and quickly ~~flies~~ flew away.

Pradeep and Kent ~~think~~ thought the play they ~~write~~ wrote was fun and exciting. They were not sure how to end it though. Did aliens actually visit Harry and Carrie's house? Was it all a dream? They knew they would have to decide before they ~~give~~ gave their play to Ms. Lucetta.

**Try It**

In the selection above, why did the spaceship fly away? Use the past tense of the verb *fly* in your answer.

Answers will vary.

97

---

To write or speak about something that is happening right now, use the **present tense**. When something has already happened, use the **past tense**. When something has not happened yet, use the **future tense**.

   **Past:** I *used* all the shampoo.
   **Present:** I *use* all the shampoo.
   **Future:** I *will use* all the shampoo.

The future tense is formed by using the word *will* with a verb. The word *will* means that something has not taken place yet, but it will happen in the future.

   Seamus *will come* home in three days.
   The plumber *will fix* the leaky pipe.
   The water *will boil* in a minute or two.
   Ms. Webster *will make* lasagna for dinner.

**Complete It**

Complete each sentence with the future tense of the verb in parentheses ( ).

1. Charlotte __will be__ a doctor when she grows up. (be)

2. Fernando __will learn__ to speak eight languages. (learn)

3. Maddy __will train__ for the Olympics. (train)

4. Travis __will find__ a cure for a serious disease. (find)

5. Akio __will photograph__ wild animals. (photograph)

6. Elena __will travel__ all around the world. (travel)

98

---

**Rewrite It**

On the line, write **PA** if a sentence takes place in the past. Write **PR** if it takes place in the present. Then, rewrite each sentence in the future tense.

Example: __PA__ The movie ended at 8:00.

   The movie will end at 8:00.

1. __PA__ The sheepdog barked at the mail carrier.

   The sheepdog will bark at the mail carrier.

2. __PR__ The gardener picks flowers from her wildflower garden.

   The gardener will pick flowers from her wildflower garden.

3. __PR__ The robin pulls a fat earthworm from the soil.

   The robin will pull a fat earthworm from the soil.

4. __PA__ A ladybug landed on Layla's shoulder.

   A ladybug will land on Layla's shoulder.

**Try It**

1. Write a sentence about someplace you have been in the past. Underline the verb.

   Answers will vary.

2. Write a sentence about where you are right now. Underline the verb.

   Answers will vary.

3. Write a sentence about somewhere you will go or something you will do in the future. Underline the verb.

   Answers will vary.

99

---

# Answer Key

---

Change a regular verb to the **past tense** by adding **ed**. If the verb already ends in **e**, just add **d**.

elect → elect**ed**    explore → explor**ed**    taste → taste**d**

If a verb ends in **y**, change the **y** to **i** and add **ed**.

study → stud**ied**    worry → worr**ied**    carry → carr**ied**

For verbs that do not follow this pattern, do not add **ed** or **d**. Instead, change the entire word.

give → gave    bring → brought    fly → flew
think → thought    write → wrote    eat → ate
say → said    grow → grew    make → made
ride → rode

The **future tense** is formed by using the word *will* with a verb. Use the future tense to write or speak about things that have not happened yet.

    Janie *will set* the table.    Armando *will help*.

**Putting It Together**
Rewrite each sentence below in a different tense. The word in parentheses ( ) tells you which tense to use.

1. Wilbur and Orville Wright dream of flying. (past)

   <u>Wilbur and Orville Wright dreamed of flying.</u>

2. The Wright Brothers will fly the first manned plane in 1903. (past)

   <u>The Wright Brothers flew the first manned plane in 1903.</u>

3. My family and I visited Kitty Hawk—the site of the first flight. (future)

   <u>My family and I will visit Kitty Hawk—the site of the first flight.</u>

4. I wrote about our trips in my journal. (present)

   <u>I write about our trips in my journal.</u>

**100**

---

Read each sentence below. In the space, write the past tense of the underlined verb.

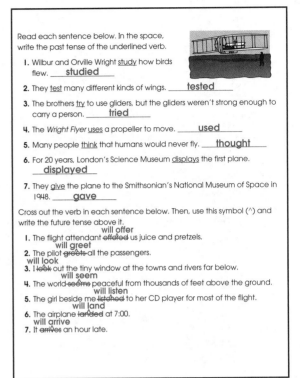

1. Wilbur and Orville Wright <u>study</u> how birds flew. <u>studied</u>

2. They <u>test</u> many different kinds of wings. <u>tested</u>

3. The brothers <u>try</u> to use gliders, but the gliders weren't strong enough to carry a person. <u>tried</u>

4. The *Wright Flyer* <u>uses</u> a propeller to move. <u>used</u>

5. Many people <u>think</u> that humans would never fly. <u>thought</u>

6. For 20 years, London's Science Museum <u>displays</u> the first plane. <u>displayed</u>

7. They <u>give</u> the plane to the Smithsonian's National Museum of Space in 1948. <u>gave</u>

Cross out the verb in each sentence below. Then, use this symbol (^) and write the future tense above it.

1. The flight attendant ~~offered~~ us juice and pretzels. **will offer**

2. The pilot ~~greets~~ all the passengers. **will greet**

3. I ~~look~~ out the tiny window at the towns and rivers far below. **will look**

4. The world ~~seems~~ peaceful from thousands of feet above the ground. **will seem**

5. The girl beside me ~~listened~~ to her CD player for most of the flight. **will listen**

6. The airplane ~~landed~~ at 7:00. **will land**

7. It ~~arrives~~ an hour late. **will arrive**

**101**

---

A **contraction** is a short way of saying something by combining two words into one. An apostrophe (') takes the place of the missing letters.

Many contractions are formed when a verb and the word *not* are combined. The apostrophe takes the place of the letter **o** in *not*.

is not = isn't    are not = aren't    was not = wasn't
were not = weren't    does not = doesn't    did not = didn't
do not = don't    can not = can't

Some contractions can be formed with pronouns and the verb *will*. An apostrophe takes the place of the letters **wi** in *will*.

I will = I'll    it will = it'll    you will = you'll
we will = we'll    she will = she'll    they will = they'll
he will = he'll

Contractions can also be made with the verb *have*. An apostrophe takes the place of the letters **ha** in *have*.

I have = I've    we have = we've
you have = you've    they have = they've

**Proof It**
Cross out the five incorrect contractions below. Use this proofreading mark (^), and write the correct contraction above it.

My neighborhood is having a giant yard sale on Saturday. ~~We'll~~ post **We'll** signs all around town. This week, ~~I'll~~ go through the boxes under my bed **I'll** and in the attic. There are many things I know we ~~do n't~~ need. At first, my **don't** little brother ~~did n't~~ want to help. Then, I told him all the money would go to **didn't** the animal shelter where we got our dog Maisy. I think ~~he ill~~ be happy to **he'll** help now.

**102**

---

**Rewrite It**
Circle the two words in each sentence that could be combined to make a contraction. Then, rewrite the sentences using contractions.

1. We (were not) even open for business yet when the first customers arrived.

   <u>We weren't even open for business yet when the first customers arrived.</u>

2. "I (will give) you 15 dollars for the tricycle," said Mrs. Smythe.

   <u>"I'll give you 15 dollars for the tricycle," said Mrs. Smythe.</u>

3. "(You will) find many great bargains," Justin told our customers.

   <u>"You'll find many great bargains," Justin told our customers.</u>

4. Our free lemonade (did not) last long.

   <u>Our free lemonade didn't last long.</u>

5. (We have) raised hundreds of dollars for the animal shelter!

   <u>We've raised hundreds of dollars for the animal shelter!</u>

6. Maisy and I (can not) wait to give the check to the shelter's director.

   <u>Maisy and I can't wait to give the check to the shelter's director.</u>

**Try It**

1. Write a sentence about something you do not like doing. Use a contraction with *not* in your sentence. Circle the contraction.

   <u>Answers will vary.</u>

2. Write a sentence about something you will do in the future. Use a contraction with *will* in your sentence. Circle the contraction.

   <u>Answers will vary.</u>

**103**

---

**Contractions** can be made with different forms of the verb *to be*. The apostrophe takes the place of the first vowel in *am, is,* and *are*.

I am = I'm
you are = you're
he is = he's
she is = she's

it is = it's
we are = we're
they are = they're

Contractions formed with the word *would* are a little different. The apostrophe takes the place of the entire word, except for the **d**.

I would = I'd
you would = you'd
he would = he'd
she would = she'd

it would = it'd
we would = we'd
they would = they'd

**Match It**

Match each pair of underlined words with its contraction. Write the letter of the contraction in the space.

1. __d__ <u>I am</u> going to take gymnastics lessons with my friend, Elise.

2. __g__ <u>She is</u> a year older than I am.

3. __b__ Elise said <u>she would</u> show me some warm-up stretches.

4. __f__ Our class meets on Wednesdays. <u>It is</u> in an old building on Fourth Street.

5. __a__ <u>We are</u> going to carpool to class.

6. __c__ Elise's dad teaches gymnastics. <u>He is</u> also the high school coach.

7. __e__ <u>I would</u> like to be on his team when I am in high school.

a. We're
b. she'd
c. He's
d. I'm
e. I'd
f. It's
g. She's

**104**

---

**Complete It**

Fill in each blank below with a contraction from the box.

| I'm | It's | He's | It'd |
|-----|------|------|------|
| We're | she'd | I'd | She's |

1. __I'd__ like to meet Olympic gold-medal gymnast Carly Patterson one day.

2. __She's__ from my hometown of Baton Rouge, Louisiana.

3. In an interview, Carly said __she'd__ like to try a career in singing.

4. Elise's favorite gymnast is Blaine Wilson. __He's__ a three-time Olympic gymnast.

5. __We're__ each going to write a letter to Carly and Blaine.

6. __I'm__ sure they will write back to us when they hear what big fans we are.

7. __It'd__ be an amazing experience to see the Olympic Games live.

8. __It's__ my dream to travel to the 2016 Olympics.

**Try It**

1. Write a sentence about a famous person you would like to meet. Use a contraction in your sentence. Underline the contraction.

   __Answers will vary.__

2. Write a sentence that includes a contraction with the word *am, is,* or *are*. Underline the contraction.

   __Answers will vary.__

**105**

---

**Negative words** are words like *no, none, never, nothing, nobody, nowhere,* and *no one*. The word *not* and contractions that use *not* are also negative words. A sentence needs only one negative word. It is incorrect to use a **double negative**, or more than one negative word, in a sentence.

**Correct:** There were *not* any oranges in the refrigerator.
There were *no* oranges in the refrigerator.
**Incorrect:** There were *not no* oranges in the refrigerator.

**Correct:** Kevin *never* saw anyone he knew at the store.
Kevin saw *no one* he knew at the store.
**Incorrect:** Kevin *never* saw *no one* he knew at the store.

**Correct:** *None* of the students were born in another country.
**Incorrect:** *None* of the students *weren't* born in another country.

**Proof It**

Read the paragraphs below. There are five double negatives. Cross out one negative word or phrase in the incorrect sentences to correct them.

If you haven't ~~never~~ heard of Jellyfish Lake, you should learn more about it. This amazing saltwater lake is in Palau, an island in the Philippines. You do not ~~never~~ want to get too close to a jellyfish in the ocean. Ocean jellyfish sting their prey. The jellyfish of Jellyfish Lake do not have ~~no~~ stingers. Instead, they use algae and sunlight to get the nutrients they need.

These jellyfish have only one predator—the sea anemone. This is why there are so many of them. No one can ~~never~~ swim in the lake without seeing millions of these jellyfish. It is a special experience for humans. ~~Not~~ <u>N</u>owhere else in the world can people swim surrounded by more than 25 million harmless jellyfish.

**106**

---

**Complete It**

Read each sentence below. Circle the word or words from the pair in parentheses ( ) that correctly complete each sentence.

1. The jellyfish don't (never, (ever)) stop moving.

2. They don't do ((anything), nothing) but follow the sun across the lake all day long.

3. My aunt said there ((is), is not) nowhere on Earth she would rather go snorkeling.

4. People who swim with the jellyfish shouldn't ((ever), never) lift or throw the delicate animals.

5. There aren't (no, (any)) jellyfish without stingers in the oceans of the world.

6. Because the jellyfish don't have to hunt for their food, there ((was), was not) no need for stingers.

7. The beautiful jellyfish don't (never, (ever)) seem to be too bothered by human visitors.

8. El Niño brought high temperatures to Palau in the late 1990s. Suddenly, there weren't ((any), no) jellyfish in the lake.

**Try It**

1. Write a sentence using one of these negative words: *no, none, never, nothing, nobody, nowhere, no one,* or *not*.

   __Answers will vary.__

2. On another piece of paper, write a sentence using a double negative. Trade papers with a classmate. On the line below, write your classmate's sentence correctly.

   __Answers will vary.__

**107**

---

# Answer Key

---

A **contraction** is a short way of saying something by combining two words into one. An apostrophe (') takes the place of the missing letters.

Some contractions are formed with a verb and the word *not*.

is not = isn't     were not = weren't     do not = don't

Other contractions are combinations of pronouns with the verbs *will, have, am, is, are,* and *would*.

we will = we'll      you have = you've      I am = I'm
it is = it's         we are = we're         you would = you'd

Do not use more than one negative word, *no, not, none, never, nothing, nobody, nowhere,* and *no one,* in a sentence. This includes contractions with *not*.

**Correct:** The Cougars *haven't* lost any games this season.
**Incorrect:** The Cougars *haven't* lost *no* games this season.

**Putting It Together**

Read the paragraph below. Cross out the five incorrect contractions. Use this symbol (^), and write the correct contractions above them. Then, find the two double negatives, and correct them.

aren't

Ghost towns ~~arent~~ the strong, lively towns they used to be. ~~The'yve~~

They've

changed because people and businesses have moved away. Most ghost

towns are in the West. Many of them used to be mining towns. When

wasn't                                                         haven't

there ~~was'nt~~ anything left to mine, the towns dried up. Towns that ~~havent'~~

don't

changed since the 1800s can be fun to explore. But ~~dont~~ expect to take

any                              anything

home ~~no~~ souvenirs. No one is allowed to take ~~nothing~~ from the towns—

except for photographs.

**108**

---

Match each pair of underlined words with its contraction. Write the letter of the contraction on the line.

1. __e__  <u>Do not</u> explore a ghost town without a map and plenty of water.

2. __b__  The guide said it <u>is not</u> a good idea to get too close to mine openings.

3. __g__  <u>She is</u> an expert in ghost towns of the West.

4. __c__  We <u>did not</u> want to miss seeing Tombstone, Jerome, and Wolf Hole.

5. __f__  <u>They are</u> located in Arizona—so are more than 250 other ghost towns!

6. __a__  <u>I have</u> put together an album of the ghost towns I have visited.

7. __d__  I think <u>you would</u> enjoy learning the histories of these deserted towns.

a. I've
b. isn't
c. didn't
d. you'd
e. Don't
f. They're
g. She's

Read each pair of sentences. Make a check mark (✓) next to each sentence that uses negative words correctly.

1. ____  Some towns don't never recover when a mine closes.
   ✓  Some towns don't ever recover when a mine closes.

2. ✓  There are not any buildings left in some abandoned towns.
   ____  There are not no buildings left in some abandoned towns.

3. ____  Dad says there isn't nowhere like ghost towns for learning about life in the Old West.
   ✓  Dad says there is nowhere like ghost towns for learning about life in the Old West.

**109**

---

The word **plural** means *more than one*. To make many nouns plural, add **s**.

one egg → two egg**s**          one dog → six dog**s**
one pencil → many pencil**s**    one photo → nine photo**s**

If a noun ends in **sh, ch, s,** or **x,** form the plural by adding **es**.

one bush → three bush**es**      one peach → five peach**es**
one fox → two fox**es**          one bus → several bus**es**

If a noun ends with a consonant and a **y,** drop the **y** and add **ies** to form the plural.

one baby → all the bab**ies**    one city → many cit**ies**

**Complete It**

Read each sentence below. Complete it with the plural form of the word in parentheses ( ).

1. Ethan made two ___wishes___ as he blew out his birthday candles. (wish)

2. All the ___branches___ in the yard came down during the huge thunderstorm last week. (branch)

3. Jacob takes care of the ___cats___ next door when our neighbors go out of town. (cat)

4. We need about six ripe ___apples___ to make apple pie. (apple)

5. Hallie left her ___glasses___ at a friend's house. (glass)

6. Claudia and Crista picked sour ___cherries___ from the tree in the yard. (cherry)

7. Please recycle the ___boxes___ in the garage. (box)

8. Four ___families___ have volunteered to organize the book sale. (family)

**110**

---

**Solve It**

Read the clues below. Find the word in the box that matches each clue. Then, make the word plural, and write it in the numbered space in the crossword puzzle.

| airplane | dress |
|----------|-------|
| bed      | beach |
| giraffe  | fox   |
| dish     | baby  |

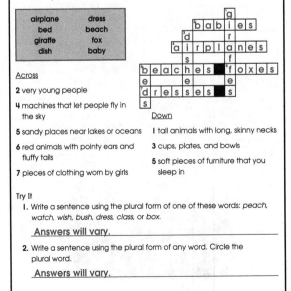

**Across**

2 very young people

4 machines that let people fly in the sky

5 sandy places near lakes or oceans

6 red animals with pointy ears and fluffy tails

7 pieces of clothing worn by girls

**Down**

1 tall animals with long, skinny necks

3 cups, plates, and bowls

5 soft pieces of furniture that you sleep in

**Try It**

1. Write a sentence using the plural form of one of these words: *peach, watch, wish, bush, dress, class,* or *box*.

   ___Answers will vary.___

2. Write a sentence using the plural form of any word. Circle the plural word.

   ___Answers will vary.___

**111**

---

Some plural words do not follow the rules. Instead of adding an ending to these words, you need to remember their plural forms.

one *man*, seven *men*      one *foot*, two *feet*
one *woman*, five *women*    one *goose*, ten *geese*
one *ox*, six *oxen*         one *child*, a lot of *children*
one *mouse*, many *mice*     one *die*, two *dice*

Some words do not change at all. The singular and plural forms are the same.

one *deer*, six *deer*        one *fish*, forty *fish*
one *moose*, two *moose*    one *sheep*, a dozen *sheep*
one *trout*, five *trout*       one *series*, three *series*
one *species*, nine *species*

**Match It**
Match each phrase below to the correct plural form. Write the letter on the line.

1. __b__ one woman     **a.** fifty womans     **b.** fifty women

2. __a__ one die        **a.** six dice          **b.** six dies

3. __a__ a moose      **a.** many moose     **b.** many mooses

4. __a__ the trout      **a.** hundreds of trout    **b.** hundreds of trouts

5. __a__ one species    **a.** eight species     **b.** eight specieses

6. __b__ the goose     **a.** four gooses     **b.** four geese

7. __b__ one ox         **a.** a herd of oxes    **b.** a herd of oxen

8. __b__ a child       **a.** most childs     **b.** most children

112

---

**Solve It**
On the lines below, write the plural form of each word in the box.

| foot | feet | ox | oxen | deer | deer |
|------|------|-----|------|------|------|
| man | men | mouse | mice | sheep | sheep |

Use the words in the box to complete the rhymes below.

1. The room was filled with 25 ____men____, and every single man's name was Ken.

2. "Hurry, hurry, hurry!" said all of the ____sheep____. "Walking's too slow, let's take the jeep!"

3. I am only one tiny gray ____mouse____, and yet there are dozens of cats in this house.

4. Please do me a favor and move your ____feet____. I do not want footprints all over my seat!

5. In the garden I see dozens of ____deer____, and they've eaten all of my lettuce, I fear.

6. The man scratched his head and looked at the ____ox____. "Was it you who ate my bagel and lox?"

7. If I've told you once, I've told you twice. There's no room in this house for any more ____mice____!

**Try It**
On the lines below, make up two of your own rhymes using one of the plurals from the exercise above.

1. **Answers will vary.**
2. **Answers will vary.**

113

---

When something belongs to a person or thing, they *possess* it. An apostrophe (') and the letter **s** at the end of a word show that the person or thing is the owner in a **possessive**.

Julianne**'s** violin        the school**'s** gym
Ichiro**'s** basketball     the tiger**'s** stripes
the park**'s** gates        Trent**'s** sister

**Proof It**
The possessives below are missing apostrophes. To add an apostrophe, use this symbol (ˇ).

1. The White Houseˇs address is 1600 Pennsylvania Avenue.

2. Two fires almost destroyed the home of the nationˇs president.

3. The Presidentˇs House, the Presidentˇs Palace, and the Executive Mansion were early names for the White House.

4. The Oval Officeˇs shape was chosen by President Taft.

5. Some of the worldˇs best artists have work displayed in the White House.

6. President Bushˇs dogs, Barney and Miss Beazley, are Scottish terriers.

114

---

**Rewrite It**
Rewrite the sentences below. Replace the underlined words in each sentence with a possessive.

Example: The capital of Hawaii is Honolulu.
     *Hawaii's capital is Honolulu.*

1. The hometown of Ronald Reagan is Tampico, Illinois.
   **Ronald Reagan's hometown was Tampico, Illinois.**

2. The nickname of Benjamin Harrison was "Little Ben."
   **Benjamin Harrison's nickname was "Little Ben."**

3. Theodore Roosevelt was the youngest president of the nation.
   **Theodore Roosevelt was the nation's youngest president.**

4. Laura Bush, the wife of the president, used to be a teacher.
   **Laura Bush, the president's wife, used to be a teacher.**

5. The 39th president of America was Jimmy Carter.
   **America's 39th president was Jimmy Carter.**

6. Before he became president, one of the jobs of Harry Truman was farming.
   **Before he became president, one of Harry Truman's jobs was farming.**

**Try It**
Write a sentence about a well-known figure from history. Use a possessive in your sentence.

**Answers will vary.**

115

# Answer Key

To form the **possessive of a plural** word that ends in **s**, add an apostrophe after the **s**.

| | |
|---|---|
| the girls' room | the monkeys' food |
| the berries' juice | the teachers' decision |

For plural words that do not end in **s**, add an apostrophe and an **s** to form the possessive.

| | |
|---|---|
| the people**'s** goals | the men**'s** clothes |

## Complete It
Read each sentence below. Replace the words in parentheses ( ) with a possessive. Write the possessive in the space.

1. (The thick white fur of polar bears) **The polar bears' thick white fur** keeps them warm during Arctic winters.

2. (The mother of the bear cubs) **The bear cubs' mother** protects her babies from wolves and other predators.

3. (The coats of caribou) **The caribous' coats** change colors, depending on the seasons.

4. (The flippers of seals) **The seals' flippers** make them strong, speedy swimmers.

5. When the young girl listened quietly, she could hear (the songs of walruses) **the walruses' songs**.

| Tip | Apostrophes are the key to telling the difference between a plural and a possessive. | |
|---|---|---|
| | **Plural** | **Possessive** |
| | thousands of bugs | a bug's wings |
| | several boys | the boys' clubhouse |
| | four watermelons | the watermelon's seeds |

**116**

---

## Identify It
Read each phrase below. If it is plural, write **PL** on the line. If it is plural possessive, write **PP**.

1. **PL** the playful baby seals
2. **PP** the igloos' walls
3. **PL** the floating icebergs
4. **PL** the Arctic rivers
5. **PL** hundreds of salmon
6. **PP** the puffins' brightly-colored beaks
7. **PP** the explorers' route
8. **PP** the people's warm clothing

## Try It
Write two sentences that include plural words.

1. **Answers will vary.**
2. **Answers will vary.**

Now, write two sentences that use the possessive form of the plural words from above.

3. **Answers will vary.**
4. **Answers will vary.**

**117**

---

To make many nouns **plural**, add **s**.

| | | |
|---|---|---|
| book, book**s** | car, car**s** | color, color**s** |

If a noun ends in **sh**, **ch**, **s**, or **x**, form the plural by adding **es**.

| | | |
|---|---|---|
| pouch, pouch**es** | kiss, kiss**es** | dish, dish**es** |

If a noun ends with a consonant and a **y**, drop the **y** and add **ies**.

| | | |
|---|---|---|
| country, countr**ies** | duty, dut**ies** | party, part**ies** |

Some irregular words don't follow these patterns.

| | | |
|---|---|---|
| man, **men** | mouse, **mice** | child, **children** |

The singular and plural forms of some words are the same. The words *deer*, *fish*, *moose*, *sheep*, *trout*, *series*, and *species* are the same in their singular and plural forms.

An apostrophe (') and an **s** at the end of a word show that a person or a thing owns something else. These words are **possessives**.

| | | |
|---|---|---|
| the jacket**'s** zipper | Eric**'s** keys | the school**'s** mascot |

To form the possessive of a plural word that ends in **s**, add an apostrophe after the **s**.

| | | |
|---|---|---|
| the cars' lights | the students' ideas | the babies' bottles |

For plural words that do not end in **s**, add an apostrophe and an **s** to form the possessive.

| | | |
|---|---|---|
| the geese**'s** feathers | the women**'s** friends | the children**'s** room |

## Putting It Together
Read the singular words below. Choose the letter of the correct plural from each pair in parentheses ( ). Write the letter in the space.

1. **b** fox (**a.** foxs **b.** foxes)  2. **a** cherry (**a.** cherries **b.** cherrys)
3. **a** calf (**a.** calves **b.** calvs)  4. **b** boss (**a.** boss's **b.** bosses)

**118**

---

Complete the sentences below with the possessive of the plural word in parentheses ( ).

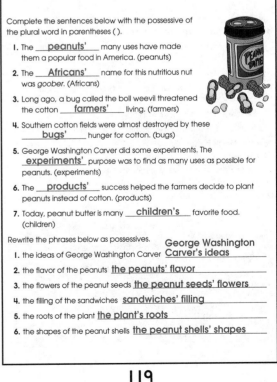

1. The **peanuts'** many uses have made them a popular food in America. (peanuts)

2. The **Africans'** name for this nutritious nut was *goober*. (Africans)

3. Long ago, a bug called the boll weevil threatened the cotton **farmers'** living. (farmers)

4. Southern cotton fields were almost destroyed by these **bugs'** hunger for cotton. (bugs)

5. George Washington Carver did some experiments. The **experiments'** purpose was to find as many uses as possible for peanuts. (experiments)

6. The **products'** success helped the farmers decide to plant peanuts instead of cotton. (products)

7. Today, peanut butter is many **children's** favorite food. (children)

Rewrite the phrases below as possessives.

1. the ideas of George Washington Carver **George Washington Carver's ideas**
2. the flavor of the peanuts **the peanuts' flavor**
3. the flowers of the peanut seeds **the peanut seeds' flowers**
4. the filling of the sandwiches **sandwiches' filling**
5. the roots of the plant **the plant's roots**
6. the shapes of the peanut shells **the peanut shells' shapes**

**119**

---

Spectrum Language Arts
Grade 3

# Answer Key

---

---

---

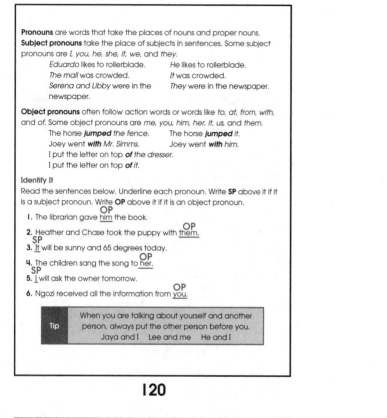
---

---

## Page 124

**Adverbs** can be used to make comparisons. Some adverbs follow the same rules that adjectives do. For most one-syllable adverbs, add **er** or **est** to make a comparison.

The boy in the blue shorts ran *faster* than I did.
Over the summer, Katherine grew *taller* than Jane.

To make a comparison using adverbs that end in **ly**, use the words *more* or *most*.

Aunt Peg read the book *more slowly* than Uncle Calvin.
My sister sang *most beautifully* of all the girls in her class.

**Complete It**
Fill in the spaces in the chart with the correct adverbs. Remember that some comparative adverbs need to be used with the words *more* or *most*.

| | | |
|---|---|---|
| slowly | __more slowly__ | most slowly |
| fast | faster | __fastest__ |
| skillfully | __more skillfully__ | __most skillfully__ |
| happily | more happily | __most happily__ |
| __patiently__ | more patiently | most patiently |
| __late__ | __later__ | latest |
| safely | __more safely__ | most safely |
| playfully | __more playfully__ | __most playfully__ |

**124**

## Page 125

**Proof It**
Read the diary entry below. There are seven comparative adverb mistakes. Cross out each mistake. To add a word, use this symbol (^) and write the correct word above it.

Saturday, September 24

Dear Diary,

Today was the first day of Flannery's obedience class. We got
there ~~soonest~~ (sooner) than most of the other dogs and owners. Flannery
sniffed and greeted the dogs as they arrived. She wagged her tail
~~most~~ (more) cheerfully than any other dog.

The class leader helped everyone teach their dogs some basic
commands. He laughed ~~more~~ harder than anyone when Flannery
stole a treat out of his pocket. I'm sure he will hide them ~~carefuller~~ (more carefully)
next time. The little dachshund standing next to us fetched ~~more~~ (most)
eagerly of all the dogs. She had short little legs, but she could run
~~more fast~~ (faster) than many of the bigger dogs. At the end of the class, Mom
and I clapped ~~most~~ loudest of all the owners! Flannery will get her
diploma in no time!

**Try It**
1. Write a sentence comparing two or more people or things. Use some form of the adverb *playfully*.

__Answers will vary.__

**125**

## Page 126

**Subject pronouns** take the place of subjects in sentences. Some subject pronouns are *I, you, he, she, it, we,* and *they*.

*Uncle John* bought a sandwich.     *He* bought a sandwich.
*Craig and Steph* skated at the park.     *They* skated at the park.

**Object pronouns** often follow action words or words like *to, at, from, with,* and *of*. Some object pronouns are *me, you, him, her, it, us,* and *them*.

Sid *told* Frank the tire was flat.     Sid *told* him the tire was flat.
Leo gave the book *to the girls*.     Leo gave the book *to them*.

Use **comparative adjectives** to compare things that are similar. Add **er** to an adjective to compare two things. Add the ending **est** to compare three or more things. If the adjective ends in **e**, just add **r** or **st**.

dark, dark**er**, dark**est**   neat, neat**er**, neat**est**   large, larg**er**, larg**est**

For adjectives that end in a consonant and a **y**, drop the **y** and add **ier** or **iest**.

silly, sill**ier**, sill**iest**   tiny, tin**ier**, tin**iest**   busy, bus**ier**, bus**iest**

For most one-syllable adverbs, add **er** or **est** to make a **comparative adverb**. To make a comparison using adverbs that end in **ly**, use the words *more* or *most*.

The plane quickly flew *higher*.
This time, she whispered *more softly*.

**Putting It Together**
Read the sentences below. Circle each pronoun. Write **SP** in the space if it is a subject pronoun. Write **OP** in the space if it is an object pronoun.

1. __OP__ Mom asked (you) to take out the trash.
2. __SP__ (They) completed the entire marathon.
3. __SP__ (It) is in the refrigerator.
4. __OP__ The e-mail is from (her).

**126**

## Page 127

Read the paragraph below. Cross out the eight incorrect pronouns. Use this symbol (^), and write the correct pronouns above them.

Last week, an exchange student named Annette came to live with
~~we~~ (us). ~~Her~~ (She) is from France. Mom is a French teacher, so ~~her~~ (she) can talk to Annette
without any problems. Dad is terrible with other languages. ~~Him~~ (He) knows a
little French, but it is hard to understand him. Annette gave ~~he~~ (him) some tips,
but it hasn't seemed to help yet. Annette is going to go to class with Mom.
Mom's students can ask ~~she~~ (her) about life in France. ~~Them~~ (They) are only allowed to
speak French to Annette, so it will be good practice for ~~they~~ (them).

Read each of the following sentences. The adjective or adverb in each sentence is in **bold** type. On the line below the sentence, write your own sentence. Use a comparative form of the same adjective or adverb.

Example: Max lifted the **heavy** boxes and put them in the moving truck.
An elephant is heavier than a horse.

1. Nina placed three **soft** pillows on the bed.
__Answers will vary.__

2. The turtle walked **slowly** to the pond.
__Answers will vary.__

3. Rory **happily** waved to his parents.
__Answers will vary.__

4. Will you show me how to make this **tasty** chili?
__Answers will vary.__

**127**

## Page 128

**Synonyms** are words that have the same, or almost the same, meanings. Using synonyms in your writing can help you avoid using the same words over and over. They can make your writing more interesting.

| quick, fast | present, gift | sad, unhappy |
| close, near | jump, hop | tired, sleepy |

**Antonyms** are words that have opposite meanings.

| old, young | wide, narrow | true, false |
| never, always | funny, serious | smile, frown |

**Complete It**

Read each sentence below. If the sentence is followed by the word *synonym*, write a synonym for the underlined word on the line. If it is followed by the word *antonym*, write an antonym for the underlined word.

1. The rocks in the walls of the Grand Canyon are millions of years <u>old</u>. (antonym) __young__

2. Limestone is the <u>top</u> layer in the nine layers of rocks. (antonym) __bottom__

3. The waters of the Colorado River formed the <u>enormous</u> canyon. (synonym) **Possible answers: huge, giant**

4. Francisco Vásquez de Coronado led the <u>first</u> Europeans to see the canyon. (antonym) __last__

5. Native Americans lived in the canyon <u>before</u> Europeans arrived. (antonym) __after__

6. If you <u>yell</u> into the canyon, you will hear echoes of your voice. (synonym) **Possible answers: scream, shout, holler**

7. People <u>like</u> taking burro rides through the canyon. (synonym) __enjoy__

**128**

## Page 129

**Solve It**

Write a synonym from the box beside each word in numbers 1–5. Write an antonym from the box beside each word in numbers 6–10.

| difficult | wrong | destroy | sleepy | giggle |
| close | cheap | speak | loose | same |

1. laugh __giggle__
2. wreck __destroy__
3. talk __speak__
4. shut __close__
5. tired __sleepy__
6. right __wrong__
7. expensive __cheap__
8. tight __loose__
9. easy __difficult__
10. different __same__

```
r t j d e g h o s q d
f d i f f i c u l t g
j e i b w g h m e y y
o s a m e g e d e u r
a t w b k l e p z n
w r o n g e p n y u e
i l o o s e k c l o s e
g y c l n s p e a k d
```

Now, find the words from the box in the word search puzzle. Circle each word you find. Words are written across and down.

**Try It**

1. Write a sentence using a synonym for *terrific*.
   __Answers will vary.__

2. Write a sentence using an antonym for *boring*.
   __Answers will vary.__

**129**

## Page 130

**Homophones** are words that sound alike but have different spellings and meanings. Here are some examples of homophones.

| Did you *hear* that noise? | The party is *here*. |
| Connor *knew* it would rain today. | I like your *new* haircut. |
| There is only *one* pancake left. | I *won* the raffle! |
| *Our* family is very large. | Pick Sam up in an *hour*. |
| *Your* mom speaks Spanish. | *You're* my best friend. |

**Identify It**

Read each sentence below. If the word in **bold** type is used correctly, make a check mark (✓) on the line. If it is not used correctly, write its homophone on the line.

1. __knew__ Mei **new** the best way to get from Seattle, Washington, to Portland, Oregon.

2. __✓__ We are meeting for lunch an **hour** before we go up in the Space Needle.

3. __Your__ **You're** sister said that it rains a lot in Seattle.

4. __✓__ The Seattle Mariners **won** the game on Friday night!

5. __Our__ **Hour** class is going on a field trip to Pike Place Market.

6. __✓__ Is **your** boat docked in Puget Sound?

7. __here__ The 1962 World's Fair was held **hear** in Seattle.

8. __new__ The **knew** Seattle Central Library is a beautiful glass and steel building located downtown.

**130**

## Page 131

**Complete It**

Read the following sentences. Complete each sentence with a word from the pair of homophones in parentheses. Write the word on the line.

1. Jada __knew__ they would take the Washington State Ferry to Bainbridge Island. (knew, new)

2. __Our__ family moved to Seattle because Mom works with computers. (Hour, Our)

3. I can see the Cascade Mountains from __here__! (hear, here)

4. I am excited that __you're__ going hiking at Mount Rainier this weekend. (your, you're)

5. __One__ of Seattle's most famous residents is computer giant Bill Gates. (Won, One)

6. Brendan did not __hear__ the guide say that Smith Tower was Seattle's first skyscraper. (hear, here)

7. The Seattle Seahawks moved into their __new__ football stadium in 2002. (new, knew)

8. Does __your__ uncle still work at the Seattle Children's Museum? (you're, your)

**Try It**

On the lines below, write two sentences. Use the word *won* in the first sentence. Use the word *one* in the second sentence.

1. __Answers will vary.__
2. __Answers will vary.__

**131**

# Answer Key

**Multiple-meaning words** are words that are spelled the same but have different meanings. Look at how the word is used in the sentence to figure out which meaning it has.

In the first sentence below, the word *trunk* means *an elephant's snout*. In the second sentence, it means *a sturdy box used for storage*.

> The elephant used its *trunk* to pick up the stick.
> Grandpa's old photos are stored in a *trunk* in the attic.

In the first sentence below, the word *fair* means *a carnival*. In the second sentence, it means *equal* or *just*.

> Jonah rode on a Ferris wheel at the county *fair*.
> It is not *fair* that I have to go to bed an hour earlier than Amanda.

**Find It**
The dictionary entry below shows two different meanings for the same word. Each meaning is a different part of speech. Use the dictionary entry to answer the questions below.

> **watch** *noun* a small device that is worn on the wrist and used to keep time
> *verb* to look at or follow with one's eyes

1. Mikayla's grandparents gave her a watch for her birthday. Which definition of *watch* is used in this sentence? __a__
   **a.** the first definition  **b.** the second definition

2. Did you watch the movie you rented? Which definition of *watch* is used in this sentence? __b__
   **a.** the first definition  **b.** the second definition

3. What part of speech is *watch* when it is used to mean *a device used to keep time?* __a__
   **a.** a noun  **b.** a verb

132

---

**Match It**
Read each sentence below. Choose the definition that matches the way the word in **bold** type is used in the sentence. Write the letter of the definition on the line.

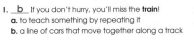

1. __b__ If you don't hurry, you'll miss the **train**!
   **a.** to teach something by repeating it
   **b.** a line of cars that move together along a track

2. __b__ Mark scored a **goal** in the second half of the game.
   **a.** something that people work hard to achieve
   **b.** a score in a game when a puck or ball is shot into a certain area

3. __a__ Eloise is the **second** child in a family of four girls.
   **a.** number two; the one that comes after the first
   **b.** a moment in time; a small part of a minute

4. __b__ We dropped pennies in the **well** and made a wish for each one.
   **a.** healthy; good
   **b.** a deep hole in the ground, used to get water or oil

5. __a__ Gabrielle's piano teacher is **patient** when she makes mistakes.
   **a.** not easily irritated or annoyed
   **b.** someone who is getting medical treatment

**Try It**
1. Write a sentence using one of the multiple-meaning words from the exercise above (*train, goal, second, well, patient*).

   __Answers will vary.__

2. Now, write a sentence using the other meaning of the word you chose.

   __Answers will vary.__

133

---

**Synonyms** are words that have the same, or almost the same, meanings.
> shut, close   friend, pal   dad, father   grin, smile

**Antonyms** are words that have opposite meanings.
> win, lose   over, under   happy, sad   asleep, awake

**Homophones** are words that sound alike but have different spellings and meanings.

> My school has a *new* cafeteria.   Raisa *knew* him long ago.
> May I have *one* cookie?   The Cavaliers *won* the game.
> *Your* shirt matches your eyes.   I think *you're* very funny.

Sometimes two words are spelled the same but have different meanings. These words are **multiple-meaning words**. Use the context of the sentence to figure out which meaning is being used.

> The *fly* landed on the food.   Will you drive or *fly* to Detroit?

**Putting It Together**
Read the following paragraphs. There are six incorrect homophones. Cross them out, and write the correct homophones above them, using this symbol (^).

"I am glad ~~your~~ you're used to hiking in the mountains," said Omar. "People who are not used to being up so high get tired quickly," he added.

"It is really beautiful ~~hear~~ here," said Nate. "I know we've been hiking for only ~~won our~~ one hour. It feels like we're miles away from the rest of the world, though."

"I ~~new~~ knew you would like this hike," replied Omar. "My family comes here every year. I'm surprised we haven't ~~one~~ won an award for Most Outdoorsy Family of the Year!"

134

---

Read each sentence below. Then, write your own sentence. If there is an **S** at the end of the sentence, use a synonym for the word in bold type. If there is an **A** at the end of the sentence, use an antonym.

1. This was the most **exciting** trip Omar and Nate had taken. **A**
   __Answers will vary.__

2. Nate sat on a rock **under** a tree to retie the laces on his boots. **S**
   __Answers will vary.__

3. Their stomachs were **empty**, but they wanted to hike until dusk. **A**
   __Answers will vary.__

4. Suddenly, Nate and Omar heard a **loud** roar. **A**
   __Answers will vary.__

5. Omar **grinned** when he saw the little boys in the bushes pretending to be bears. **S**
   __Answers will vary.__

Choose the sentence in which the word in **bold** type is used the same way as it is in the first sentence. Write the letter of your answer in the space.

1. __a__ Saki swung the **bat** as hard as she could.
   **a.** Ted has a new baseball **bat**.   **b.** The **bat** ate a bug.

2. __b__ The tree's **leaves** are changing color.
   **a.** Dad **leaves** at 8:00.   **b.** Aimee raked the **leaves**.

3. __a__ Grandpa used the power **saw** to cut the wood.
   **a.** The **saw** is in the tool chest.   **b.** I **saw** you at the movies.

135